1st EDITION

Perspectives on Modern World History

The Fall of the Berlin Wall

1st EDITION

Perspectives on Modern World History

The Fall of the Berlin Wall

Jeff T. Hay

Book Editor

GREENHAVEN PRESS

A part of Gale, Cengage Learning

Detroit • New York • San Francisco • New Haven, Conn • Waterville, Maine • London

Christine Nasso, *Publisher*
Elizabeth Des Chenes, *Managing Editor*

For more information, contact:
Greenhaven Press
27500 Drake Rd.
Farmington Hills, MI 48331-3535
Or you can visit our Internet site at gale.cengage.com

Articles in Greenhaven Press anthologies are often edited for length to meet page requirements. In addition, original titles of these works are changed to clearly present the main thesis and to explicitly indicate the author's opinion. Every effort is made to ensure that Greenhaven Press accurately reflects the original intent of the authors. Every effort has been made to trace the owners of copyrighted material.

LIBRARY OF CONGRESS CATALOGING-IN-PUBLICATION DATA

The fall of the Berlin Wall / Jeff T. Hay, book editor.
p. cm. -- (Perspectives on modern world history)
Includes bibliographical references and index.
ISBN 978-0-7377-4558-0 (hardcover)
1. Berlin Wall, Berlin, Germany, 1961-1989--Juvenile literature. 2. Berlin (Germany)--Politics and government--1945-1990--Juvenile literature. 3. Cold War--Juvenile literature. I. Hay, Jeff.
DD881.F33 2010
943'.1550877--dc22 2009027493

Printed in the United States of America
1 2 3 4 5 6 7 13 12 11 10 09

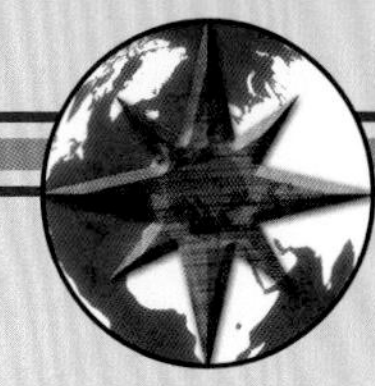

CONTENTS

CHAPTER 3 Watching the Wall Come Down

FOREWORD

"History cannot give us a program for the future, but it can give us a fuller understanding of ourselves, and of our common humanity, so that we can better face the future."

—Robert Penn Warren, American poet and novelist

The history of each nation is punctuated by momentous events that represent turning points for that nation, with an impact felt far beyond its borders. These events—displaying the full range of human capabilities, from violence, greed, and ignorance to heroism, courage, and strength—are nearly always complicated and multifaceted. Any student of history faces the challenge of grasping the many strands that constitute such world-changing events as wars, social movements, and environmental disasters. But understanding these significant historic events can be enhanced by exposure to a variety of perspectives, whether of people involved intimately or of ones observing from a distance of miles or years. Understanding can also be increased by learning about the controversies surrounding such events and exploring hot-button issues from multiple angles. Finally, true understanding of important historic events involves knowledge of the events' human impact—of the ways such events affected people in their everyday lives—all over the world.

Perspectives on Modern World History examines global historic events from the twentieth-century onward by presenting analysis and observation from numerous vantage points. Each volume offers high school, early college level, and general interest readers a thematically arranged anthology of previously published materials that address a major historical event, with an emphasis on international coverage. Each volume opens with background information on the event, then presents the controversies surrounding that event, and concludes with first-person narratives from people who lived through the event or were affected by it. By providing primary sources from the time of the event, as well as relevant commentary surrounding the event, this series can be used to inform debate, help develop critical thinking skills, increase global awareness, and enhance an understanding of international perspectives on history.

Material in each volume is selected from a diverse range of sources, including journals, magazines, newspapers, nonfiction books, personal narratives, speeches, congressional testimony, government documents, pamphlets, organization newsletters, and position papers. Articles taken from these sources are carefully edited and introduced to provide context and background. Each volume of Perspectives on Modern World History includes an array of views on events of global significance. Much of the material comes from international sources and from U.S. sources that provide extensive international coverage.

Each volume in the Perspectives on Modern World History series also includes:

- A full-color **world map**, offering context and geographic perspective.
- An annotated **table of contents** that provides a brief summary of each essay in the volume.
- An **introduction** specific to the volume topic.
- For each viewpoint, a brief **introduction** that has notes about the author and source of the viewpoint, and that provides a summary of its main points.
- Full-color **charts**, **graphs**, **maps**, and other visual representations.

- Informational **sidebars** that explore the lives of key individuals, give background on historical events, or explain scientific or technical concepts.
- A **glossary** that defines key terms, as needed.
- A **chronology** of important dates preceding, during, and immediately following the event.
- A **bibliography** of additional books, periodicals, and Web sites for further research.
- A comprehensive **subject index** that offers access to people, places, and events cited in the text.

Perspectives on Modern World History is designed for a broad spectrum of readers who want to learn more about not only history but also current events, political science, government, international relations, and sociology—students doing research for class assignments or debates, teachers and faculty seeking to supplement course materials, and others wanting to improve their understanding of history. Each volume of Perspectives on Modern World History is designed to illuminate a complicated event, to spark debate, and to show the human perspective behind the world's most significant happenings of recent decades.

INTRODUCTION

In late 1989 the famous American composer Leonard Bernstein traveled to Berlin to conduct a performance of Beethoven's Ninth Symphony. The symphony's fourth movement is a choral known as the "Ode to Joy," in which singers emphasize, often in dramatic terms, the German word *freude*, or "joy." For this performance, Bernstein planned to replace *freude* with *freiheit*, the German word for "freedom." He was certain that Beethoven's great symphony, with this one small but important alteration, would provide a fitting celebration of one of the key events of recent world history: the fall of the Berlin Wall.

The Berlin Wall had stood for nearly 30 years, and during that time it was the most visible symbol of the Cold War. While there were very elaborate and sometimes dangerous borderlines separating nations around the world, Berlin, the former and present-day capital of Germany, was the only city on earth actually divided by a barrier made up of concrete blocks, electrified wire, guard towers, and, in some areas, a dangerous no-man's land of open territory stretching away from its eastern side. It was, indeed, the world's most obvious border.

The Berlin Wall was designed to keep people in, not to keep people out. Those whose free movements were thus restricted were the residents of East Germany as well as those of other Eastern European Communist nations such as Poland, Czechoslovakia, Hungary, Romania, and Bulgaria. Those nations had become Communist in the late 1940s when, in the aftermath of the World War II victory over Nazi Germany, the Soviet Union sought to build a buffer of friendly Communist regimes in the nations that separated it and the Western European powers. The Soviet Union was aided in this regard by its massive armed services, known familiarly as the Red Army, which were already in place across Eastern Europe when Nazi Germany fell in 1945.

In various post–World War II agreements, the Allied powers, which had defeated Nazi Germany, decided to divide the nation into four separate zones of occupation in order to return stability, as well as a new government, to the nation. The United States, the Soviet Union, Great Britain, and France each had a zone of occupation in this arrangement, which was intended to be only temporary. The Allied powers also agreed to divide Berlin itself up into four zones, despite the fact that it lay entirely within the zone of Germany designated to fall under Soviet control.

As relations between the Soviet Union and the Western powers, notably the United States, deteriorated into the long, tense Cold War, Berlin's situation stabilized, but in an extremely unusual way. By 1949, the three western zones of occupation were being transformed into a free democratic state known familiarly as West Germany. The Soviets, meanwhile, planted friendly German Communists into positions of power in their zone, ultimately creating Communist East Germany. Berlin itself was likewise divided; East Berlin emerged as the capital of East Germany while West Berlin remained an outpost of the free world surrounded by Communist states.

By the late 1950s, many Eastern Europeans were taking advantage of the existence of this outpost to escape to the West. Many of these exiles were highly educated or skilled, and so this wave of refugees constituted a "brain drain" from East to West. It was in order to close off this escape route, as well as to address the threat represented by, they claimed, "Western militarism and fascism," that East Germany's leaders announced stricter border controls, which were ultimately to include the Berlin Wall, in August of 1961. From then on it was very difficult for ordinary people to travel from East to West. Some, those who tried to cross without official permission, were killed in the attempt. The first of these was 18-year-old Peter Fechter, who was shot by border guards and then left to die in the wall's shadow in August 1962.

Eventually somewhere between one hundred and two hundred people (figures are in dispute) died trying to cross the wall illegally. As many as five thousand, however, managed the attempt successfully. Meanwhile, eight gates in the wall made possible occasional visits on the part of Germans and a few others, though such visits required special permits. The gate most famous in the United States was the one known as Checkpoint Charlie, which was the only one open to Western military personnel or, surprisingly, the occasional tourist willing to exchange a certain amount of valuable West German currency for its virtually worthless East German counterpart.

While the wall itself remained bleak and forbidding on the eastern side, many of its lengths on the western side were decorated with graffiti or other forms of public art. Indeed, as the wall remained in place, Berliners grew used to its existence and learned how to live with it, even as it remained an obvious sign of the intolerance and repression of Communist East Germany.

Then, in December 1988, the Soviet leader Mikhail Gorbachev announced, to the world's surprise, that the Red Army's presence in Eastern European countries was to be reduced substantially. In the same period, and into 1989, Hungary and Czechoslovakia began making it easier for people to travel from those countries to West Germany. As their predecessors had in the 1950s, many East Germans took advantage of these new openings to try to escape. When the East German government cracked down, massive public protests erupted. In the face of these, leaders announced the lifting of border restrictions between East and West Germany, including those along the Berlin Wall. The new state of affairs would begin the night between November 9 and 10, 1989. At this point, Berliners began to take matters into their own hands, moving freely across the barrier, taking part in large, spontaneous public celebrations, and quickly taking hammers to the wall itself. By the end of 1989 the Communist regime in East Germany was in tatters, and in 1990 the two Germanys were united once again, with a whole Berlin as its capital. Communism in Eastern Europe as a whole collapsed quickly, until by the end of 1991 even the Soviet Union was beginning the transition to democracy or some other, non-Communist form of government.

The fall of the Berlin Wall remains the greatest symbol of these rapid and unexpected changes. Leonard Bernstein's performance of Beethoven's Ninth, complete with its resounding cries of *freiheit*, was a vivid part of the celebration of the rebirth of freedom across Eastern Europe. The performance was held in a concert hall in the former East Berlin and broadcast over the radio to an audience of an estimated 100 million. It took place on Christmas Day 1989, a mere six weeks after the Berlin Wall ceased to have meaning except as a reminder of recent history.

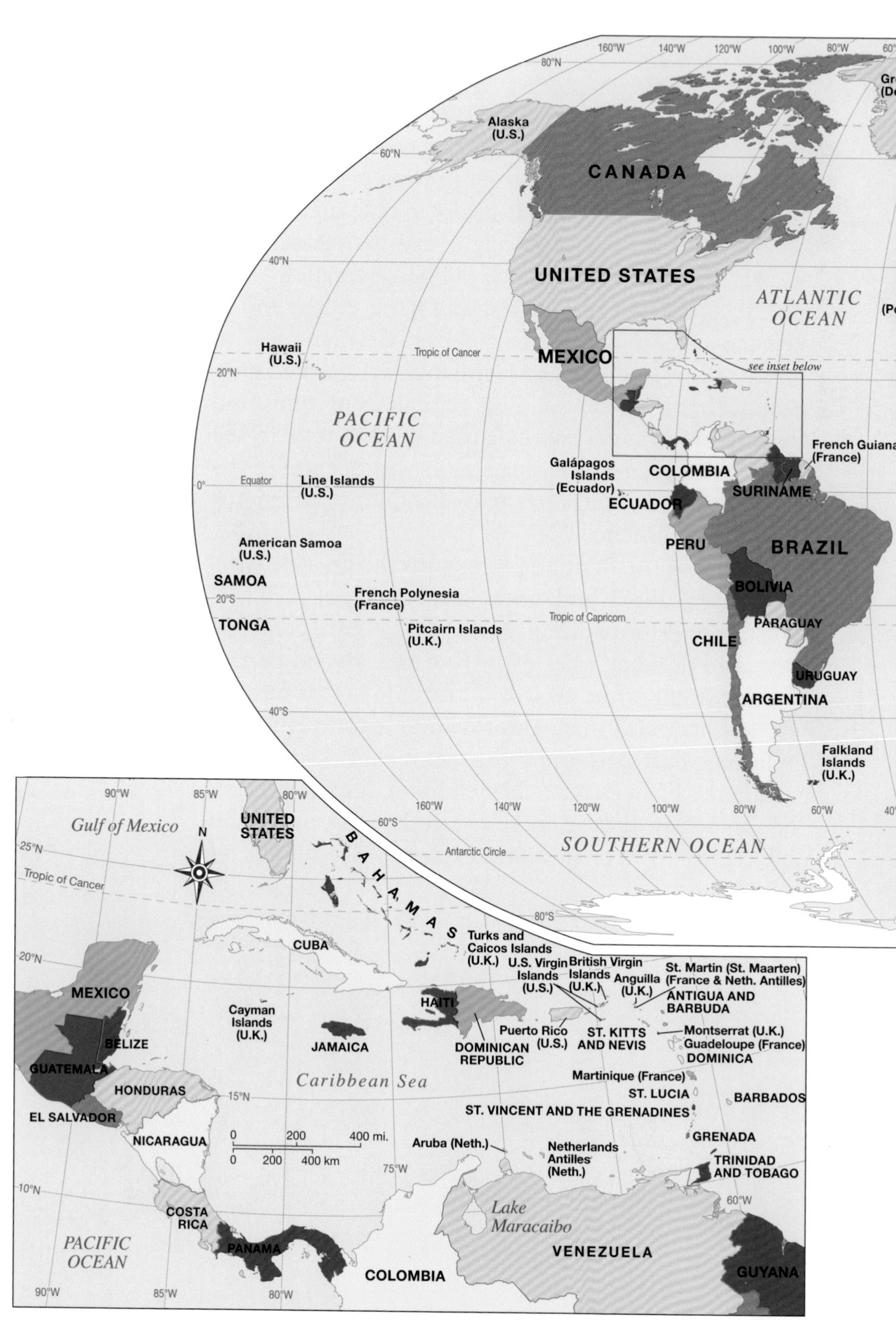

Alaska (U.S.)
CANADA
UNITED STATES
ATLANTIC OCEAN
MEXICO
Hawaii (U.S.)
Tropic of Cancer
see inset below
PACIFIC OCEAN
Galápagos Islands (Ecuador)
COLOMBIA
French Guiana (France)
SURINAME
Equator
Line Islands (U.S.)
ECUADOR
American Samoa (U.S.)
PERU
BRAZIL
SAMOA
BOLIVIA
French Polynesia (France)
TONGA
Tropic of Capricorn
PARAGUAY
Pitcairn Islands (U.K.)
CHILE
URUGUAY
ARGENTINA
Falkland Islands (U.K.)
SOUTHERN OCEAN
Antarctic Circle
Gulf of Mexico
UNITED STATES
BAHAMAS
Tropic of Cancer
Turks and Caicos Islands (U.K.)
CUBA
U.S. Virgin Islands (U.S.)
British Virgin Islands (U.K.)
Anguilla (U.K.)
St. Martin (St. Maarten) (France & Neth. Antilles)
ANTIGUA AND BARBUDA
MEXICO
HAITI
Cayman Islands (U.K.)
Puerto Rico (U.S.)
ST. KITTS AND NEVIS
Montserrat (U.K.)
Guadeloupe (France)
BELIZE
JAMAICA
DOMINICAN REPUBLIC
DOMINICA
GUATEMALA
Caribbean Sea
Martinique (France)
HONDURAS
ST. LUCIA
BARBADOS
EL SALVADOR
ST. VINCENT AND THE GRENADINES
NICARAGUA
0 200 400 mi.
0 200 400 km
Aruba (Neth.)
Netherlands Antilles (Neth.)
GRENADA
TRINIDAD AND TOBAGO
COSTA RICA
Lake Maracaibo
PACIFIC OCEAN
PANAMA
VENEZUELA
GUYANA
COLOMBIA

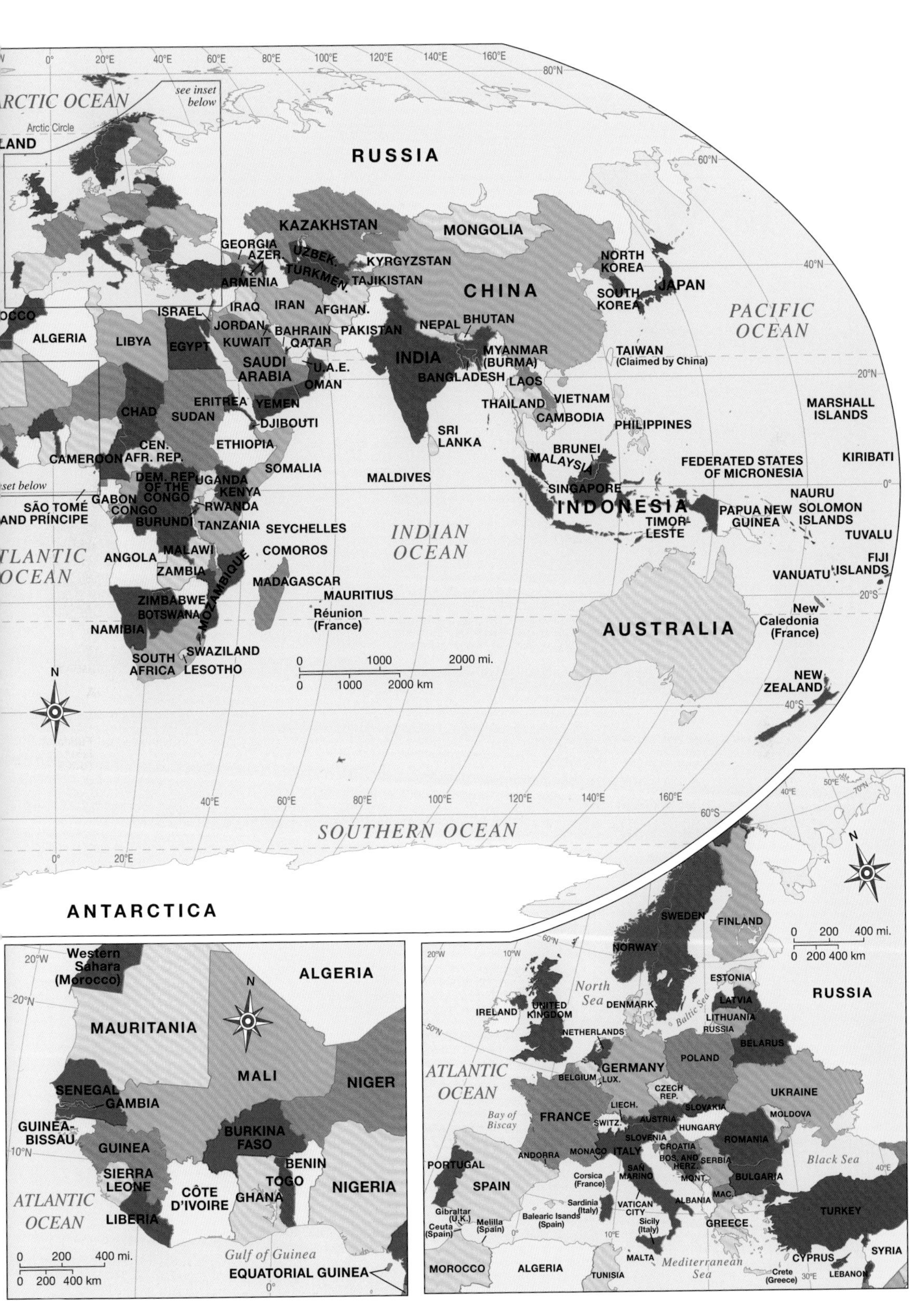

RUSSIA
KAZAKHSTAN
MONGOLIA
GEORGIA
AZER.
ARMENIA
UZBEK.
TURKMEN.
KYRGYZSTAN
TAJIKISTAN
CHINA
NORTH KOREA
SOUTH KOREA
JAPAN
PACIFIC OCEAN
ISRAEL
IRAQ
IRAN
AFGHAN.
JORDAN
BAHRAIN
KUWAIT
QATAR
PAKISTAN
NEPAL
BHUTAN
ALGERIA
LIBYA
EGYPT
SAUDI ARABIA
U.A.E.
OMAN
INDIA
MYANMAR (BURMA)
BANGLADESH
TAIWAN (Claimed by China)
LAOS
VIETNAM
THAILAND
CAMBODIA
PHILIPPINES
CHAD
SUDAN
ERITREA
YEMEN
DJIBOUTI
ETHIOPIA
SRI LANKA
MARSHALL ISLANDS
CEN. AFR. REP.
CAMEROON
SOMALIA
BRUNEI
MALAYSIA
FEDERATED STATES OF MICRONESIA
KIRIBATI
DEM. REP. OF THE CONGO
UGANDA
KENYA
MALDIVES
SINGAPORE
NAURU
GABON
CONGO
RWANDA
BURUNDI
TANZANIA
SEYCHELLES
INDONESIA
PAPUA NEW GUINEA
SOLOMON ISLANDS
SÃO TOMÉ AND PRÍNCIPE
TIMOR-LESTE
TUVALU
ATLANTIC OCEAN
ANGOLA
MALAWI
COMOROS
INDIAN OCEAN
ZAMBIA
MOZAMBIQUE
FIJI ISLANDS
VANUATU
MADAGASCAR
MAURITIUS
ZIMBABWE
BOTSWANA
Réunion (France)
NAMIBIA
AUSTRALIA
New Caledonia (France)
SOUTH AFRICA
SWAZILAND
LESOTHO
NEW ZEALAND
SOUTHERN OCEAN
ANTARCTICA
Arctic Circle
see inset below
ARCTIC OCEAN
0 1000 2000 mi.
0 1000 2000 km
Western Sahara (Morocco)
ALGERIA
MAURITANIA
MALI
NIGER
SENEGAL
GAMBIA
GUINEA-BISSAU
GUINEA
BURKINA FASO
BENIN
SIERRA LEONE
TOGO
NIGERIA
CÔTE D'IVOIRE
GHANA
LIBERIA
ATLANTIC OCEAN
Gulf of Guinea
EQUATORIAL GUINEA
0 200 400 mi.
0 200 400 km
SWEDEN
FINLAND
NORWAY
ESTONIA
RUSSIA
North Sea
DENMARK
LATVIA
IRELAND
UNITED KINGDOM
Baltic Sea
LITHUANIA
RUSSIA
NETHERLANDS
BELARUS
POLAND
GERMANY
BELGIUM
LUX.
ATLANTIC OCEAN
CZECH REP.
UKRAINE
LIECH.
SLOVAKIA
MOLDOVA
FRANCE
AUSTRIA
Bay of Biscay
SWITZ.
HUNGARY
SLOVENIA
ROMANIA
CROATIA
ANDORRA
MONACO
ITALY
BOS. AND HERZ.
SERBIA
Black Sea
PORTUGAL
SAN MARINO
MONT.
BULGARIA
SPAIN
Corsica (France)
MAC.
ALBANIA
Sardinia (Italy)
VATICAN CITY
TURKEY
Gibraltar (U.K.)
Ceuta (Spain)
Melilla (Spain)
Balearic Isands (Spain)
Sicily (Italy)
GREECE
MALTA
Mediterranean Sea
CYPRUS
SYRIA
MOROCCO
ALGERIA
TUNISIA
Crete (Greece)
LEBANON

CHAPTER 1

Historical Background on the Berlin Wall

VIEWPOINT 1

The Division of Germany and the First Crises in Berlin

Richard C. Hanes, Sharon M. Hanes, and Lawrence W. Baker

The city of Berlin changed quickly from being the capital city of Nazi Germany, a criminal state responsible for much of the devastation of World War II (1939–1945), to serving as the center point of the Cold War in Europe. The following selection traces that transition, examining how the powers that had vanquished Nazi Germany—the United States, the Soviet Union, Great Britain, and France—had different expectations and plans for the defeated state. The Soviet Union in particular, having suffered greatly from the war and professing a Communist ideology, hoped to spread communism to parts of Germany and to exploit it economically.

The victorious powers divided Germany into four zones of occupation, one each for Britain, France, the United States,

Photo on previous page: During the period that preceded the raising of the wall in Berlin, barricades and signs indicated borders between the city's international zones. **(Carl Mydans/ Time Life Pictures/Getty Images.)**

SOURCE. Richard C. Hanes, Sharon M. Hanes, and Lawrence W. Baker, *Cold War Reference Library, Volume 1: Almanac, Gale Virtual Reference Library*. Detroit, MI: U*X*L, 2004.

and the Soviet Union. Likewise, Berlin itself was divided into four sectors though physically the city stood entirely within the Soviet zone of occupation. Plans to govern the whole using a four-power Allied Control Commission fell apart as the Soviets sought to instill communism in their zone while the Western powers hoped to revive Germany's economy and build democratic institutions. By 1948, the Western powers began to take steps to rule western Germany—their zones—independently. The Soviets responded by blockading Berlin, attempting to force the Western powers out of the city by closing all land and water routes to it.

As the selection indicates, the Western powers managed to preserve their presence in Berlin by supplying it by air for nearly a year, a remarkable logistical achievement. This Berlin airlift helped to harden the division of the city as well as the German nation, and by the end of 1949, two Germanys existed. One was the Federal Republic of Germany (FRG), made up of the three western zones and governed from the Rhineland city of Bonn. The other was the Communist German Democratic Republic (GDR), governed from East Berlin. In the West, the two were commonly referred to simply as West Germany and East Germany.

On May 7, 1945, Germany surrendered to the Allies in Reims, France, bringing an end to World War II (1939–1945) in Europe. The "Big Four" allies were the United States, Great Britain, France, and the Soviet Union. Allies are alliances of countries in military opposition to another group of nations. Immediately upon Germany's surrender, an Allied plan that divided Germany into four zones became effective. Each zone was occupied by troops from one of the Big Four countries; each country appointed a military governor to oversee its zone. Within a few years, the democratic U.S., British, and French zones were col-

> At the end of the war, the cities of Germany lay in ruin.

The Soviet blockade of Berlin in 1948 was among the most significant crises the city faced in the years after World War II and before the building of the wall in 1961. (Popperfoto/Getty Images.)

lectively referred to as West Germany. The communist Soviet zone became known as East Germany.

Although Germany's capital, Berlin, was located well within the Soviet zone, the four Allies divided the capital city into four sectors, in the same way as they had divided the whole of Germany. The same four Allied powers each occupied a sector of Berlin. The U.S., British, and French sectors soon became known as West Berlin. The Soviet-occupied sector was called East Berlin. Road, rail, water, and air routes running from West Germany through and over East Germany to Berlin made trade possible. The three Western powers identified specific trade and supply routes from West Germany into Berlin and expected the Soviets to grant free access to Berlin through these corridors.

Different Points of View

At the end of the war, the cities of Germany lay in ruin. The British Royal Air Force and the U.S. military had relentlessly released bombs on German targets. Particularly in the last year of the war, bombs rained down on Germany day and night, and Berlin was not spared. Many of Berlin's stately buildings were reduced to shells and rubble. One-third of Berlin's population, approximately 1.5 million people, had fled or had been killed. The urgent task of governing a shattered Germany fell to the four Allied powers. Yet each of the four powers had differing points of view on how to deal with postwar Germany. From the start, neither negotiations nor cooperative efforts among the four proceeded smoothly.

> "American leaders believed a strong democratic Germany could stop the westward spread of communism."

The Soviet Union had suffered greatly at the hands of the invading Germans. The Soviets strongly opposed rebuilding Germany's economic base. They did not want to fear another German invasion in the future, as they had experienced on several occasions in the past. Throughout 1946 and 1947, the Soviets demanded billions of dollars in reparations from Germany—repayment for the heavy damage German troops had inflicted on their country. Within the Soviet zone of Germany, they disassembled entire factories that had not been damaged by the war and shipped the equipment to Russia for reassembly.

The Soviet Union operated under a communist government. Communism is a system of government in which a single party controls almost all aspects of society. In theory, a communist economy eliminates private ownership of property so that goods produced and accumulated wealth are shared relatively equally by all. At the war's end, the Soviet Union immediately began expanding its influence into the Eastern European countries it occupied by establishing communist governments. Included was Poland, which lay between the Soviet Union's western boundary and Germany. The Soviets also established communist governments in their zone of Germany (East Germany) and in the Soviet sector of Berlin (East Berlin). In these regions of Germany, the entire economic base—factories, banks, and farms—was seized and organized under the communist system. The Soviets appointed German communists to leadership positions in local government offices.

The United States believed that controlling Germany and deliberately keeping the German people in an impoverished state (as a result of reparations) would only breed defiance . . . and lead to more struggles in the future. In conflict with Soviet wishes, the United States wanted to end reparations and rebuild a strong democratic Germany with a capitalist economy. A democratic system of government consists of several political parties whose members are elected to various government offices by a vote of the people. In a capitalist economy, property can be privately owned. Prices, production, and distribution of goods are determined by competition in a market relatively free of government intervention. The United States was becoming increasingly concerned about the Soviets' rapidly expanding communist influence in Europe. American leaders believed a strong democratic Germany could stop the westward spread of communism.

> Germany became a focal point of the Cold War.

Badly damaged during the war and still resentful of Germany's wartime aggression, Great Britain somewhat reluctantly agreed that a democratic Germany with a revitalized economic base could be essential for a strong democratic and capitalist Western Europe. Britain held the key to Germany's revitalization because the Ruhr River region was part of the British-occupied zone. This region was home to large coal mining operations and the great iron and steel factories where cars and machinery were manufactured. Britain and the United States soon agreed on rebuilding Germany; both countries also favored dissolving the four zones to make one united Germany.

France did not want to rebuild Germany any more than the Soviets did. France had been invaded by the Germans three times in the twentieth century alone. The French people dreaded the prospect of a strong, reunited Germany. Nevertheless, given the choice of aligning with the communist Soviet Union or the Western democratic nations of the United States and Britain, France moved to the democratic side, reluctantly dropping its opposition to rebuilding Germany.

Focal Point of the Cold War

The Cold War was usually not fought on battlefields with large armies; it was a conflict between the ideologies, or political orientations, of the communist Soviet Union and the democratic, capitalist Western nations. Because of its geographic position between Western Europe and the Soviet Union, Germany became a focal point of the Cold War.

By early 1948, the three Western powers were making plans to unite their occupied zones of Germany, both economically and politically. They also planned to unite their sections of Berlin. In February, leaders from the United States, Britain, and France, along with representatives of Belgium, the Netherlands, and Luxembourg, met in London to discuss a new West German state. Having well-placed spies, the Soviet Union knew of the meeting. The Soviets believed that the proposed West German state would pose a military and political threat to the

The Battle of Berlin

As the capital of Adolf Hitler's Nazi Germany, the city of Berlin was an important target for the Allied nations of the United States, Great Britain, and the Soviet Union. The major contribution of the U.S. and Britain to the conquest of Berlin was through bombing raids. It was left to the Soviet Union to subdue the city on the ground.

The British launched their first bombing raids on Berlin in 1940, although these caused little damage. Once the United States entered World War II in late 1941, and once longer-range bomber planes were available, the raids increased. The last major Allied air attacks on Berlin were from February to April 1945. In their entirety these attacks killed thousands, rendered even more homeless, and left much of the city in ruins.

Meanwhile, the Soviet Union's Red Army launched a major ground attack on Berlin in early April 1945. Their attack force included some 2.5 million men, over 6 thousand tanks, and tens of thousands of artillery pieces and rocket launchers. Russian guns, indeed, destroyed more of the city than British and American bombs had.

Hitler refused to either surrender or be taken alive, and he committed suicide on April 30, 10 days after the Soviet artillery attacks began. Remaining German military forces surrendered piecemeal, and by early May, the city was in Soviet hands. The German capital, formerly a scene of imperial glory, was now one of miles and miles of rubble full of hungry, humiliated, and terrorized citizens.

The overall commander of Allied forces in the west, General Dwight D. Eisenhower, had no interest in sending American or British troops to Berlin, since the city had already been left within the postwar Soviet Zone of Occupation. Little did Eisenhower know that future agreements would divide the city itself.

Soviet zone of Germany and the Soviet Union itself. When the Allied Control Council, an organization of military governors from each of the four zones, met in March, the Soviet delegation accused the Western-sector governors of conspiring against the Soviet Union and walked out of the meeting. This action brought an end to the Allied Control Council, the only organized body of all four occupying powers.

Within weeks of the Allied Control Council meeting, the Soviets began harassing train, automobile, and water traffic coming from the West German zones into Berlin. Soviet officials began randomly searching passengers and inspecting cargo on trains destined for Berlin. Restrictions popped up on automobile routes and river traffic routes. Soviet fighter planes called Yak-3s harassed planes on scheduled flights from West German air bases to Berlin. On April 5 a Yak-3 collided with a British European Airways transport plane, killing eleven people. Tensions escalated rapidly.

Berlin Blockade

On June 18, 1948, a quarrel over German currency increased tensions even further. Unable to reach agreement with the Soviets on ways to stop German inflation (a rapid increase in consumer prices), the Western powers issued new currency in the western zones of Germany. For the moment, the new currency, called the deutsche mark (D-mark), was not issued in Berlin. Replacing the worthless reichsmark, the new currency had been secretly printed in the United States by the U.S. Mint. Soviet officials immediately rejected the new currency and moved that day to close off all automobile, rail, and water traffic into Berlin from the western zones. On June 23, the Soviets introduced into the Soviet zone—and into all of Berlin—the ostmark. Soviet authorities insisted that all of Berlin use the ostmark, because all sectors of Berlin were within the Soviet zone of Germany. However, the Western powers rejected the ostmark and introduced the deutsche mark in West Berlin. In response, at dawn on June 24, the Soviets halted all shipments of supplies and food through East Germany into West Berlin. They cut all coal-generated electricity supplied from East Germany to Berlin's western sectors, and

ZONES OF OCCUPATION:
POST-WORLD WAR II GERMANY AND BERLIN, 1947

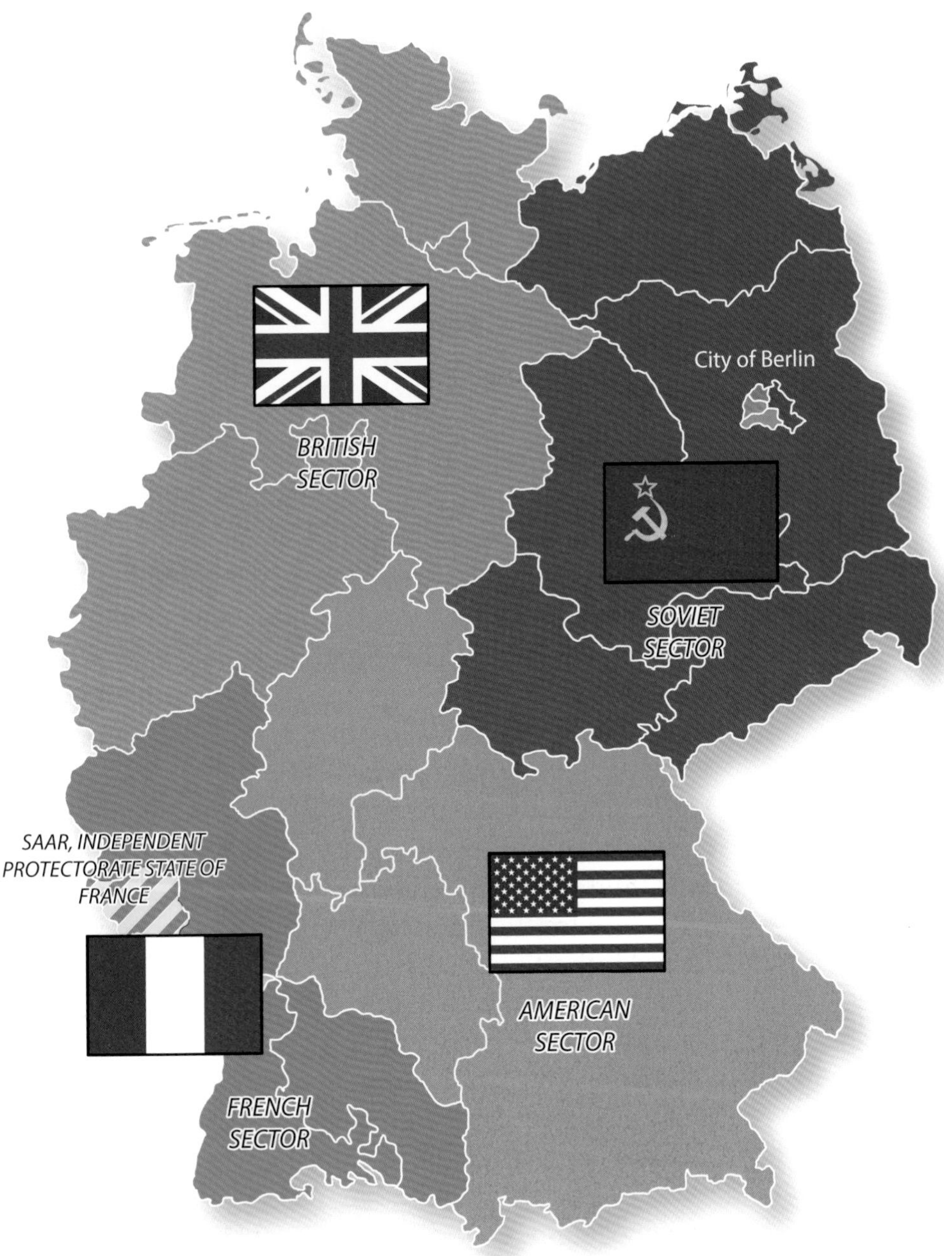

Taken from: WikiNight, Wikimedia Commons, Creative Commons Attribution ShareAlike 3.0.

land and water routes from West Germany into Berlin were closed. The 2.3 million Berliners living in the western sectors of the city, as well as the military personnel stationed there, were marooned within Soviet-controlled territory. A total blockade was in place.

Berlin Airlift

The Soviets hoped the blockade would force the Western powers to leave Berlin. Above all else, the Soviets wanted to prevent West Berlin from becoming part of the newly proposed West German state, because they feared that the Western powers might place U.S. atomic weapons in West Berlin, right next door to Soviet-controlled territory. The Soviets also hoped that the blockade would weaken the spirit of West Berliners, so that they would agree to communist rule. These hopes were dashed by a massive airlift organized by the Western powers. Rather than abandoning the city, they sent the British Royal Air Force (RAF) and the U.S. Air Force in Europe (USAFE) to fly the necessities of life into West Berlin. . . .

The United States nicknamed the airlift Operation Vittles, and the British dubbed the effort Operation Plain Fare. At first, two airfields in Berlin were used, Tempelhof in the U.S. sector and Gatow in the British sector of the city. Volunteer German workers—men and women—labored to build a third airport, Tegel, in the French sector. (Tegel would receive its first supply missions on November 5.) By mid-July, the airlift was delivering nearly 2,000 tons (1,814 metric tons) of supplies a day, including the first shipments of coal.

Also in July, with much publicity, the United States sent three B-29 bomber squadrons (sixty aircraft) to England to stress how determined the Western allies were to resist Soviet pressure. The B-29s were capable of carrying atomic bombs and were within easy reach of the Soviet Union. The bombers carried no atomic weapons, but the Soviet government was kept guessing.

In early September, three hundred thousand West Berliners gathered to demonstrate for continuance of the airlift. Seven thousand tons of cargo arrived on September 18. In mid-October, U.S. and British aircrews joined forces under a unified command, the Combined Airlift Task Force, headquartered in Wiesbaden in the U.S. zone of Germany. Flights landed every ninety seconds at Tempelhof and Gatow, often in bad weather conditions. Pilots flew exacting patterns at specified speed and altitude. They were locked into patterns so tight that if an aircraft failed to land on the first attempt, it had to return to West Germany rather than make a second attempt.

By spring 1949, the Soviets had lost hope that the airlift would fail. West Berliners neither starved nor froze but instead adjusted to supplies arriving by airlift. The West Berlin economy actually began to grow. By spring, 8,000 tons (7,256 metric tons) per day was the average delivery. Stockpiles grew. April 16 was the record day for deliveries: Known as the "Easter Parade," 1,398 flights brought 12,940 short tons (11,700 metric tons) of cargo. (A short ton is 2,000 pounds; a long ton is 2,240 pounds.) The successful airlift was a huge propaganda victory for the Western powers. Propaganda is facts and ideas deliberately circulated to promote one's own cause or to damage the opposing side's cause.

At midnight on May 12, 1949, the Soviets stopped the blockade and reopened highway, train, and water routes into West Berlin. (The airlifts, however, would continue through September 30, 1949.) The city's residents began to celebrate; they—and many others around the world—hoped that the Cold War had come to an end.

Further Separation of West and East Germany

The Western allies allowed West German officials to craft their own constitution, approved on September

> In 1955, West Germany became . . . [an] independent nation.

21, 1949, which combined the three West German zones into the Federal Republic of Germany. The new West German parliament selected Bonn as West Germany's capital. The West German people elected Konrad Adenauer (1876–1967), the chairman of the country's Christian Democratic party, as their first chancellor. Aided by the Marshall Plan, U.S. funding assistance for economic recovery and development, the West German economy was revitalized and began to thrive. In 1955, West Germany became a completely independent nation. That year it also joined the North Atlantic Treaty Organization (NATO), a Western military alliance for mutual protection.

In the Soviet-controlled zone of Germany, a communist-crafted constitution was approved on October 7, 1949. Under the new constitution, East Germany became the German Democratic Republic (GDR); its capital was East Berlin. Communist Walter Ulbricht (1893–1973) headed the East German government. Although it remained under strong Soviet influence, East Germany officially became independent of the Soviet Union in 1955. The Western powers consistently refused to recognize East Germany as an independent country.

Meanwhile, Berlin remained divided into the four sectors originally established after World War II. However, the three sectors occupied by the Western allies operated as one, both politically and economically. The Soviet sector remained under communist control.

VIEWPOINT 2

The Berlin Wall Goes Up: August 1961

David Tulloch

In the following selection, author David Tulloch examines the historical framework within which the Berlin Wall was built. The city of Berlin, the former capital of united Germany, became the flashpoint of the Cold War in Europe after 1948. Divided administratively into two cities, one the capital of Communist East Germany and the other an awkward appendage of democratic West Germany, Berlin remained an uncertain place in the late 1940s and 1950s. But, as Tulloch indicates, West Berlin served as a window by which refugees could escape East Germany, a major source of concern for Communist officials. It was to stem this tide of refugees, as well as to finally settle unfinished political business from the immediate post–World War II era, that East German officials and their Communist allies in the Soviet Union decided to build a wall separating the city's two sectors.

David Tulloch is the author of a number of articles on the history and practice of espionage.

SOURCE. David Tulloch, *Encyclopedia of Espionage, Intelligence, and Security, Vol. 1, Gale Virtual Reference Library*. Detroit, MI: Gale, 2004.

In the early hours of August 13, 1961, the border crossings between the eastern Soviet Occupied Zone of Berlin and the western American, British and French controlled sectors began to be sealed. At first barbed wire was used to separate East from West Berlin, but over time this was replaced by concrete slabs and a deadly no man's land that became known as the Berlin Wall. The Wall split a city, a people, and the world, tearing apart families and friends for decades, and becoming a powerful symbol of the Cold War, representing the deepening divide between East and West, physically, politically, and philosophically.

> "The 'Berlin Problem' . . . was also beginning to surface."

After the Second World War

Well before the D-Day invasion of mainland Europe, the three main Allied powers, Britain, the United States, and the Soviet Union, held high-level discussions to determine how to administer Germany after it had been defeated. Eventually it was decided that Germany would be split into four administrative zones, one each for the Soviets, the Americans, the British, and the French. Berlin, as the German capital, was also to be divided into four administrative zones. However, Berlin was located deep within the zone allocated to the Soviets, 180 kilometres (110 miles) from the western zones, and this geographical fact was to haunt post-war Germany for many decades.

Immediately after the war, the major concerns of the administrative powers were feeding the populace, and coping with the severe winter of 1947. The major political discussions were disagreements over the amount of reparations Germany could pay while still leaving it with sufficient resources for recovery. However, the "Berlin Problem," as it came to be known, was also beginning to surface.

Post-war military rule by the four powers was intended to be a short term measure, as it was assumed a suitable German civilian government would be quickly formed, and the Allies would then sign a peace treaty with this new authority and withdraw their troops. As a result, there was little or no long-term planning in regards to the peculiar problems of Berlin. Access routes from the Western zones were only tenuously agreed upon with the Soviets. The notion that both Germany and Berlin would remain divided for an extended period was just not considered. When relations between the Soviet Union and the Western powers began to deteriorate, all sides found themselves with a geographical problem that caused political problems.

The Cold War Heats Up

The first major crisis between East and West regarding post-war Germany began on June 24, 1948, when Western land access to Berlin was blocked by the Soviets. Berlin relied on shipments of almost every good its population used, from food and medicine to coal for heating and power generation. At first it appeared that the Western powers would be forced to either abandon their sectors of Berlin, or open a land passage to Berlin through military confrontation, risking a possible Third World War. Unexpectedly, however, it proved possible to supply Berlin with the bare essentials (and no more) through a massive airlift operation. The New York Treaty of May 4, 1949 effectively ended the Berlin blockade, and the Western counter-blockade, and supplies quickly returned to normal levels.

> There remained a steady stream of Germans who left the East of the country and resettled in the West.

The blockade effectively ended the charade of four power cooperation in the administration of Germany and Berlin, with the Soviet sector eventually becoming the German

Democratic Republic (GDR) and the Western sectors eventually becoming the Federal Republic of Germany (FRG). In both cases, however, Berlin was considered the capital city of these new countries, but a Berlin divided between the Soviets and the West. The events of the blockade were also a fundamental impetus behind the formation of the North Atlantic Treaty Organisation (NATO), and its Eastern counterpart, the Warsaw Pact, further defining the divisions of the Cold War.

Refugees

The 1950s saw both sides of Berlin turned into political and social showrooms for the competing doctrines. West Berlin developed into a capitalist Mecca, while the East of the city transformed into a model socialist city. While the border between the two areas was sealed in 1952, this did not stop half a million people crossing the borders each day. Many East Berliners worked in the West, where they could make more money and so enjoy a higher standard of living than those working in the East, a situation that led to resentment from some. Berliners from the West enjoyed the extra spending power their currency offered in the East, crossing the border for less expensive haircuts, clothes, and other goods and services. Relatives living on opposite sides of the city could visit each other, students crossed to attend schools and universities, and many people crossed the border to attend concerts and sporting fixtures. There were some measures introduced to make crossing the border difficult and frustrating, such as police controls on many crossing points, and the barricading of some streets, but over 80 access points still remained open, and the underground railway (S-bahn) still crossed regularly.

However, there were a large number of people crossing from the East who simply did not return. Towards the end of the Second World War there had been a flood of refugees fleeing from the East to the West ahead of

the advancing Soviet army. While the tide slowed after the end of the war, there remained a steady stream of Germans who left the East of the country and resettled in the West. It is estimated that more than two and a half million East Germans fled into the West between 1946 and 1961, yet the entire population of East Germany was only 17 million. The East German authorities attempted to restrict their citizens crossing by introducing passes and making "fleeing to the Republic" a crime with potential jail sentence of up to four years.

Erected in stages, the Berlin Wall evolved from stretches of barbed wire to more solid materials such as concrete. **(Volkmar K. Wentzel/National Geographic/Getty Images.)**

There were many factors driving the refugees. Some were as basic as seeking a better job, more food, or more material goods. The numbers of refugees spiked upwards during times of hardship in the East, when food and other essential resources were scarce. The social and political changes that had taken place in the Soviet zone, such as the educational reforms and the removal of many judges

> When Berliners awoke on the morning of August 13 [1961] their city had been split in two.

from their positions, resulted in many educated and wealthy persons moving to the West. The refugee problem grew and became an embarrassment for both sides. The East viewed those leaving as traitors and the West could not cope with the scale of the human tide. In the first seven months of 1961, over 150,000 East Germans left for the West. Walter Ulbricht (1893–1973), the leader of East Germany, repeatedly requested that he be able to take radical measures to stop the problem, but he was denied, at least for the time being.

The Berlin Crisis

Aside from the refugee problem, there were political troubles that threatened not only the peace and stability of Berlin and Germany, but also the world. In 1958, the Soviet Leader, Nikita Khruschev (1894–1971) demanded that several thorny post-war issues be resolved within a six-month period. The Soviets wanted negotiations on European security, an end to the four-power occupation of Germany, a final peace treaty signed with a reconstituted Germany, and the creation of a nuclear-free Germany to act as a buffer zone between the two superpowers.

The Soviets threatened that if their demands were not met then they would sign a separate peace treaty with East Germany, officially splitting Germany in two (even if in practice it already was so.) Summit talks were held in Geneva (May–August 1959), Paris (May 1960), and with the newly elected President John F. Kennedy (1917–1963) in Vienna (June 1961), but no agreements were forthcoming.

On the night of August 12, 1961, on the Eastern side of Berlin, large numbers of army units, militiamen, and People's Police (Vopos) began to assemble near the border. Beginning shortly after one in the morning the troops were posted along the border, and the wire and posts were deployed to seal East from West Berlin. Traffic was prevented from crossing, including the underground railway trains. When Berliners awoke on the morning of August 13 their city had been split in two.

The closure of the border between the two halves of Berlin came as a surprise to Western intelligence agencies. After the fact, a number of reports and individuals surfaced claiming to have foreseen the events of August 13, but at the time there was no credible source that was believed by the West. Some historians have suggested there was an overload of information at the time, with too many spies and informers supplying information. Sorting through the sheer volume of reports was one problem, as well as sorting the useful signals from the noise of half-rumor and disinformation. Reports from civilians who noticed that something "big" was occurring before the border was sealed were dismissed, as they were considered less reliable than the professional spies and informers. Credit must also be given to the secret planning and execution of Ulbricht, Erich Honecker (1912–1994), and their forces, who managed to stockpile 40 kilometres of barbed wire and thousands of posts without arousing suspicion. Even as the border was being sealed, many people on both sides had no idea what the ultimate purpose was, including those laying out the barbed wire.

> The border fencing off West Berlin from East Germany was 155 km. (96 mi.) in length.

The initial Western lack of response was baffling to many, who expected a more aggressive approach from the Western military in Berlin. The Kennedy administration appeared to accept that the Soviets had a natural right to protect their borders, and the other Western leaders followed his lead. Despite the fact that the East German actions violated the agreements the Four Powers had made after the Second World War, the United States only protested in a feeble manner. While Kennedy has been criticized heavily by biographers and historians for doing nothing, in effect, the lack of an active Western response stabilized the situation. While tension remained high for the next two years, the walling of the Berlin border did not threaten to boil over into armed conflict in the same manner as the Berlin Blockade had done.

If there had been too much intelligence information before the Wall, after the border was sealed there was the opposite problem. Before the Wall, spies crossed as easily as anyone else did. The massive tide of refugees that moved to West Berlin before the sealing of Berlin caused many intelligence problems, as it was simply not possible to effectively screen all potential communist agents when the numbers crossing were high. After the wall, it became much harder to send spies across the border, simply because there was no longer any civilian traffic. Potential spies were now much easier to spot, and security forces on both sides could now shadow all suspected persons in official parties who crossed the divide.

From Barbed Wire to Concrete

Over the years, the East Germans modified and added to the initial barbed wire fence between the two Berlins. As soon as it became obvious that the West was not challenging the erection of the barricades, the first concrete sections were moved into place. Within the first few months, the Wall began to take on a more permanent shape, consisting of concrete sections and square blocks. Weak points were quickly identified and sealed. In mid-1962, modifications were made to strengthen the Wall, and in 1965, a third generation of Wall building began, using concrete slabs between steel girders and concrete posts. The last major reconstruction of the Wall began in 1975, when interlocking concrete segments were used.

The border fencing off West Berlin from East Germany was 155 km. (96 mi.) in length. The actual concrete structure that became infamous was only 107 km. (66.5 mi.) in length, the remainder of the border was sealed off by wire and fences. More than 300 watch towers were built along the border, as well as 105 km. (65 mi.) of anti-vehicle ditches, more than 20 concrete bunkers, and all patrolled by several hundred dogs and more than ten thousand guards.

While the Wall was a formidable barrier that did not stop many East Germans from trying to cross it. In the first few days and weeks of its construction there were many gaps in the border. Escapees jumped, burrowed, climbed, and swam their way through weak points in the fence. Some East German residents lived in apartments that had windows and doors that opened into the West. Some fled to West Berlin simply by walking through their front doors, and when they were sealed, by climbing out the windows. Over time the holes and weak points in the Wall were found and blocked. Those attempting to escape in later years faced many more hazards, and while some were successful, many were wounded or killed in the attempt.

VIEWPOINT 3

The Children of West Berlin Understand That They Are Different from Those in the East

Thomas Davey

In the 1980s, child psychologist Thomas Davey traveled to West Berlin to examine the lives of children living there. By that time the Berlin Wall had been up for more than 20 years, and tens of thousands of children had grown up in the divided city, but they could not view the situation as a normal one. As the selection indicates, Davey finds that West Berlin's children commonly view those in the East, who share a similar language and heritage and might live only yards way, as being rather different from them. They express this feeling in ways ranging from jokes to sympathy. Davey also notes that, for these children, the wall is a continual reminder of Germany's past and of the uncertain

---

SOURCE. Thomas Davey, *A Generation Divided: German Children and the Berlin Wall*. Durham, NC: Duke University Press, 1987.

present in ways that it could not be to children living in West Germany proper.

Thomas Davey is a licensed psychologist practicing in the Boston area.

Several studies conducted throughout West Germany suggest that fewer and fewer Germans are willing to express pride in their nation. To the question "Are you proud to be German?" posed in 1981, only 35 percent of those questioned answered "definitely." Of those under thirty, only 20 percent answered likewise. Of those under thirty who said they were definitely proud to be German, only 26 percent would consider leaving their

Action taken in the 1953 uprising in East Berlin provided children in West Berlin with a rare connection to Germans across the wall. (**AP Images.**)

country to live elsewhere, while of those who did not feel proud of their nationality, 49 percent would gladly leave their country. Clearly . . . West Berlin children are not alone in their very mixed allegiance to their homeland.

Yet I spoke with several children who, though well aware of the particularly shameful aspects of German history, maintained a more defensive posture in the face of the Wall and its antecedents [causes], as well as adverse reactions voiced by outsiders. Twelve-year-old Michael expressed his views this way: "I know if it wasn't for Hitler, Germany would probably still be one nation today. I know he started the war and that he killed a lot of Jews. That is terrible. But he also did good things for the country; there wasn't so much 'Kaos' then like there is now, and not so many demonstrations. And people had jobs, too." This last issue is very important to Michael, as his father is out of work and has been for several months. He continues:

> Sometimes I get really sick to my stomach when we drive by the Wall. I don't usually see it, because we live near Tegel [airport], it's easy to forget it's there. I think I am used to it; but sometimes I wonder if I'll ever get used to it. Why is it there? I'm not even sure who built it; but I think they did "over there." But I'm not sure why they did. I just know if it wasn't for Hitler, there would probably be no Wall. And when tourists see the Wall, they probably think of Hitler and of how bad Germany was. But Hitler wasn't just bad; and we're not just bad either. I just try to remember the good things; this is my country, and I know it's not just the way tourists see it.

For most of these children it is simply impossible to ignore the past. It faces them squarely every time they want to drive out of the city or take a walk in the outlying countryside: the Berlin Wall. How they come to terms with that past varies from child to child. Yet most of these children acknowledge, often quite hauntingly, that it does matter a good deal to them what sort of a country they belong to and, consequently, what sort of people *they* are.

> Boris sees the people of East Germany as 'trapped' by the Russians.

And it is that kind of inquiry—who am I? What do I stand for?—that requires children to look carefully not only to the past, but to the present as well. Given the dramatic political circumstances that inform their lives, they cannot help but look around, ask questions pertaining to their situation, and arrive at some conclusions. Naturally their attention is frequently drawn to the Wall, because of the ways in which it restricts their lives and, perhaps more importantly, because of the way it hides from view the city of East Berlin and that world of state socialism.

Understanding a Divided City

For many West Berlin children, East Berlin remains an enigma [mystery], the sheer face of the Wall draws their vision toward the East yet denies satisfaction, veiling that which it highlights. The impression that most children have of East Berlin and the GDR [German Democratic Republic, or East Germany] consists of various facts acquired in school or through the media, personal observations made during border crossings and the subsequent car or train rides through East German countryside, or in moments spent peering from one of the numerous viewing platforms adjacent to the Wall. Some draw upon family stories told in the home or, for those children with relatives in the East, personal experience of life "over there." All children rely, too, on a liberal dose of imagination. Thus East Berlin is not only the object of fairly realistic appraisals made by West Berlin's children; like the Wall itself, it serves as a blank screen of sorts, on which children can project particular wishes and fears of a political, psychological, and moral nature.

Who are these people who live their lives hidden from view by the Wall? Following are two statements made by a pair of West Berlin boys, each twelve years old. They use remarkably different terms in defining their particular relationship with their neighbors to the east, and in so doing they reflect the two most frequently heard views held by the West Berlin children with whom I spoke.

> West Berlin belongs to the FRG [Federal Republic of Germany, or West Germany] and East Berlin belongs to Russia. But the people over there are like us. We were all Germans once—same religion, same ideas, same language. The Russians built the Wall because doctors were all coming over to the West where they could make more money and travel wherever they want. Over there people are trapped; I feel sorry for them. —Boris
>
> For me, Germany is the Federal Republic. The East is *no* Germany—absolutely no country as far as I'm concerned. Maybe an in-between country. I cannot understand the people over there. I understand the language but not the meaning. They are foreigners to me, just like the Turks here in Berlin. If the Wall were gone, then I would understand them. —Carsten . . .

Boris recognizes a certain kinship with the residents of the GDR, based not only on immediate family ties but on certain qualities that might be considered more "abstract": religion, ideas, language. He indicates that it is these very qualities that bring a people together and that any division of those people, at least in the case of Germany, can only be instigated from without (by the Russians). Boris sees the people of East Germany as "trapped" by the Russians, against their will; as such, they are deserving of his sympathy and concern. It is this ability to trace the connections between these two nations that allows Boris, and other children like him, to locate some sense of shared nationality beneath the confines of ideology. Often this ability is enhanced when a child has relatives "over there," such as eleven-year-old Ilke: "Why do they [the Allies] have to occupy us, like the Russians do the GDR? We should be rejoined with the people over there. It's not fair. We all have relatives over there; and we should be able to live together. We are all Germans."

> 'Sometimes we go to the observation platforms along the Wall and shout at them.'

Of course, this is the message many of these children receive not only from their parents and their own experience of visiting or being visited by grandparents from the East, but from their teachers. They are reminded often of their relation to and responsibility for their "fellow" Germans in the East. Since the war's end, and the subsequent division of Germany, the guiding vision of West German political life and Ostpolitik [policy toward East Germany] has been the hope of reunification. The most important holiday in West Berlin has been the *Tag der deutschen Einheit*, the Day of German Unity, which commemorates the workers' uprising in East Berlin on June 17, 1953. On that day workers all over the GDR put down their tools to demonstrate against excessively high production quotas; and the Soviet Union retaliated violently. Although most children are not at all sure about the significance of the day, they welcome it as a school holiday. However, children who do have close ties with relatives in the East and those who in some other manner manage to feel a strong connection to the "other" German state often speak of reunification as the bringing together of a family that has been forcefully divided. . . .

Sometimes this strong sense of a basic difference turns into cause for casting aspersions [false or misleading charges] on the East. What is not entirely understood is, at times, hated. "We call them *Ostschweine* (east pigs) over there. Sometimes we go to the observation platforms along the Wall and shout at them." Yet not all of this hostility is projection elicited by mystery. Some children have direct experience with life in the GDR, primarily through relatives living there. Others have direct experience of the particular horror of the Wall, as they live in direct proximity to it. Following is a brief account by twelve-year-old Brigitte, who lives in the working class district of Kreuzberg in direct sight of the Wall. The facts of her story were reported in newspaper accounts, as are all such events.

> I can see the Wall from my living room window. Yes, I forget about it sometimes, because it's always there. I was born here, and always remember the Wall being there. When I was little we used to play "border patrol" down there, but now I don't spend much time near it. Sometimes we hear their jeeps going by in "no-man's-land," and at night their alarms go off if someone tries to escape, or maybe they just have practice in case someone tries to escape.
>
> Well, two weeks ago someone did try. It was at night, and it's usually pretty quiet here—when all of a sudden I heard a lot of guns being fired over there. I knew someone was trying to get over, and I started to pray that he would make it. But I knew he wouldn't, and I felt so bad for him. A lot of people heard it too, and they got up and went to the Wall and started shouting and cursing at them over there. My mother let me go out with her and I shouted too. Then we started bringing garbage and other stuff over to the Wall and we set it on fire and let the wind blow the stinking smoke over to them. Everyone was so angry and some people were crying. I still wonder who it was that night; his family must be so sad. It's not fair, how they can't leave if they want to. And now I just hate the GDR, for what they do to the people.

This was an extremely powerful experience for Brigitte, and one that is not shared by many of her peers. Yet many children have an experience or two that, in similar ways, crystallize their attitudes toward the East. These experiences may fuel their anger and lead to a complete rejection of the system *and* people "over there."

These feelings frequently are conveyed through jokes. Kids say that the abbreviation for the *Deutsche Demokratische Republik*, DDR, stands for "*drei doofe Russen*" (three stupid Russians) or "*d*eutsche *D*achel*r*ennbahn" (German dachshund raceway). The joke going around during my visit referred to Erich Honecker, president of the GDR, returning to East Berlin from a trip abroad. He is surprised, as no one comes to greet him at the airport. In the city he is further taken aback, as there are no crowds cheering him along Karl Marx Allee. Thoroughly perplexed, he heads toward his office; on his way he notices a small hole in the Wall. On arriving at his office he finds a note on his desk: "You're the last one out, Erich. Be sure to turn out the lights." There is not always much laughter at this joke, but children will tell it over and over. The joke also gets told by East Berlin children, and there it is freighted with a different significance. Although various negative experiences with the GDR may cause children to totally reject that nation and its people, they may, as in Brigitte's case, force them to distinguish between government and people like themselves and encourage a more ambivalent response toward East Germany.

East Berliners Celebrate the City's 750th Anniversary

Paul Gleye

By the late 1980s, Germany had been divided formally into two nations for nearly forty years and the Berlin Wall had been up for nearly thirty years. Both city and wall, indeed, continued to serve as the greatest symbols of the Cold War and of a Europe divided into a free, lively, capitalist West and a dreary (from the Western perspective) Communist East, full of totalitarian states inhabited by a quiet, subdued, deprived populace.

Thanks to a lessening of Cold War tensions after 1985, Western travelers could visit the East with greater ease than in earlier periods, and they sometimes found that life there was not as bland as had been reported. One, scholar Paul Gleye, is the author of the following selection. In it, he reports how the population of East Germany, while generally obedient to its authorities in pursuit of building a socialist state, finds its own ways to voice protests on issues of concern such as housing

---

SOURCE. Paul Gleye, *Behind the Wall: An American in East Germany, 1988–1989*. Carbondale, IL: Southern Illinois University Press, 1991.

and the ability to migrate to the West. They use the occasion of Berlin's 750th anniversary, a state-sponsored holiday, to make their creative protests known.

Paul Gleye is a professor of architecture at North Dakota State University.

Anniversaries were . . . very important days in East Germany, tracked carefully and used to advantage in taking another step toward advanced socialist society. An important day might be a milestone anniversary of a city's founding, say 750 years, or the anniversary of an event in history deemed important for socialist history, as the 450th anniversary of the German Peasant War when farmers rose up against feudal landlords, or the anniversary of a significant event in German cultural history such as the 300th anniversary of Johann Sebastian Bach's birth in Eisenach.

Berlin's big birthday celebration a few years ago demonstrates how the anniversary system was incorporated into state planning goals. Berlin had been founded in the year 1237, and the city's 750th anniversary was coming up in 1987. It was important to make the city look good for the occasion, especially since West Berlin, being also Berlin, was celebrating the same birthday. The competition was on to see who had the best Berlin: the one on the east side of the Wall or the one on the west. The eastern one, by the way, was always "Berlin, Capital of the DDR [*Deutsche Demokratische Republic*, or East Germany]." Just as you do not call it [San Francisco] Frisco, you never called it "East Berlin." The other one, the one shown as a blank on East German maps of Berlin, was known as "Westberlin," usually written as one word.

> To have a dwelling in Berlin opened up many possibilities.

Each of the fifteen administrative regions in East Germany had its own WBK. The WBK was an

Construction workers' benefits from East Berlin housing policies struck some East Germans as unfair. (Ralph Crane/Time Life Pictures/Getty Images.)

industrialized housing construction conglomerate, or *Wohnungsbaukombinat*, charged with building new multifamily housing in its region. For several years in preparation for Berlin's 750th, the WBKs in each of the outlying fourteen regions (Berlin was its own region) were given a construction quota in East Berlin. Each was required to divert a certain percentage of its output to

Berlin—ship the materials and provide the workers to construct housing in the capital city. East Berlin was to become a showplace for socialist housing. This and other diversions of productive capacity, which had in fact continued even after the 1987 birthday, managed to worsen conditions in the rest of the country, as needed housing was not provided and needed goods were not available. The government published a handsomely illustrated booklet, "The Regions Build in Berlin," to show off their work, but many people expressed bitterness about the policy—even East Berliners, for some of whom the city seemed to be growing out of control.

Among the primary beneficiaries of the policy apparently were construction workers themselves who came from the outlying districts to build in Berlin. Since there was a housing shortage in the capital, the first dwellings they built in Berlin tended to be their own. They would live in these dwellings while building others, intending eventually to return home and free the dwellings for Berliners. In reality many remained permanently, since economic opportunities there were better than in the provinces. Under socialism one did not evict tenants from dwellings, and since availability of a dwelling was the chief practical determinant of where one could work, to have a dwelling in Berlin opened up many possibilities.

A Better Life in East Berlin

Living in East Berlin had an additional advantage. The city was flooded from across the Wall by the programs of Radio Free Berlin, rather Radio Free Westberlin (*Sender Freies Berlin*) and of RIAS (Radio in the American Sector)—despite its name a fully German station—so that one was better informed. These two influential West Berlin radio stations not only provided East Berliners with news about the world outside the Zone, they also broadcast more meaningful news about developments inside East Germany itself than did the Party-controlled DDR stations.

In further preparation for the 750th birthday of the capital city, East Germans were asked to place "Berlin 750 Years" stickers on their cars. Some people, displeased at the decree that the country should show solidarity for building up its capital at the expense of other regions where housing needs were often greater, placed their own stickers on their cars. These said things like "Dresden 780 Years," or "Leipzig 970 Years." Such behavior was not deemed sufficiently societally committed, however, and police proceeded to remove the non-Berlin bumper stickers.

Such displays on one's automobile were often a popular instrument of subtle protest. In rear windows one frequently saw stuffed ALF dolls (the beloved critter from the American television show), or the banners of West German soccer teams. A favorite sticker on the back of the diminutive Trabant automobile was the international black and yellow "long vehicle" sign. Many people who had requested permission to emigrate to West Germany tied white streamers on their car antennas as their own expression of solidarity. Those whose applications had been denied often displayed black streamers. A friend deadpanned that people who had requested emigration to the Soviet Union would display red streamers. In October of 1988, however, the People's Assembly passed a new law that prohibited attaching anything to the antenna of a car.

VIEWPOINT 5

East Berlin Protesters Demand Democratic Reforms

Democracy Now Movement

In the late 1980s the two Russian words *perestroika* and *glasnost* became familiar around the world. They were introduced into common usage by Soviet leader Mikhail Gorbachev, who took office in 1985 and wanted to bring fundamental reforms to his country. By "perestroika" he meant restructuring, mainly of the Soviet economy. By "glasnost" he meant openness in both communications and politics. One effect of Gorbachev's call for such reforms was more widespread, and louder, demands for greater democracy in both the Soviet Union and its Eastern European satellite states such as East Germany.

The following selection is a flier distributed in East Berlin in September 1989 by a group calling for democratic reforms in East Germany. Its authors cite the reforms already underway in other Communist nations and argue that East Germany's

---

SOURCE. The Democracy Now Movement, *Uniting Germany: Documents and Debates, 1944–1993*. Providence, RI: Berghahn Books, 1994.

governing party, the National Front, should test its support using open elections. The flier appeared in a time when Gorbachev had pledged to stop supporting such governments as East Germany's with Soviet military might. It was also a sample of wider protests; the Berlin Wall came down two months after its appearance.

Dear friends, fellow citizens, and all concerned!

Our country is living in a state of internal strife. Some have rubbed themselves sore under the current conditions, and others have simply resigned themselves. A great loss of approval of what has his-

The Year of Miracles

The fall of the Berlin Wall was the climax of a "Year of Miracles" that ended communism in Eastern Europe. Soviet leader Mikhail Gorbachev's surprise announcement in December 1988 that the USSR's military presence in Eastern Europe would be greatly reduced set off a wave of popular reform that long had been building.

In Poland, the protest movement and labor union known as Solidarity convinced leaders to accept a bicameral legislation and open elections in March 1989. In June, Solidarity candidates overwhelmingly defeated Communist ones. The first non-Communist government in Eastern Europe since the late 1940s took office in September.

Hungary transformed itself peacefully as well, as the Communist party that had governed it for decades reorganized itself as a milder, socialist party ready to take part in multiparty elections. The first of these was in October 1989.

Witnessing events elsewhere, the citizens of the Czechoslovakian capital of Prague demonstrated in the streets in large numbers in November, beginning what came to be known as the Velvet Revolution. Unwilling or unable to face them down, Czechoslovakia's Communist party gave up power on November 28. Open elections in December raised to the office of president the playwright and longtime dissident Vaclav Havel.

torically developed in the GDR [German Democratic Republic, or East Germany] is sweeping the country. Many can hardly justify living here any longer. And many are leaving the country because there are limits to how much conformity one can stand.

Until a few years ago, "real existing socialism" was considered the only option available. It was characterized by a centrist state party enjoying a power monopoly, state control of the means of production, state-organized infiltration and uniformity of society, and the inability of citizens to participate in their affairs. Despite its unquestionable accomplishments in terms of public welfare and social justice, it is now obvious that the era of state social-

In Bulgaria, a pro-democracy movement grew more assertive as the Communist leadership grew more inept. Demonstrations and reform demands beginning in November resulted in free and open elections in 1990.

Only in Romania did the transition result in violence. The nation's Stalinist dictator, Nicolae Ceaucescu, refused to even consider the reforms then sweeping his Eastern European neighbors. Ceaucescu's army, at first, obeyed his order to shoot protesters. But on December 22, the military shifted to support the reformers. The dictator and his wife, unable to escape, were quickly tried and executed, on local television, on December 25.

In East Germany, great civil unrest followed the government's decision to close its borders to Czechoslovakia after thousands took advantage of new freedoms to migrate west. When the borders were lifted again in early November, the Czechs provided no barrier to East Germans going first to their country and then to West Germany. Accepting the new reality, East German leaders, whose time in power would not last past December, announced the lifting of Berlin's border restrictions as of November 9. At that point, and as they had and would continue to do elsewhere in Eastern Europe, ordinary people took the reigns of reform and swept away the Berlin Wall.

> The . . . leadership has not shown any willingness to change.

ism is coming to an end. A peaceful, democratic renewal is necessary.

Introduced and emphasized by [Soviet leader Mikhail] Gorbachev, democratic reconstruction of society is underway in the Soviet Union, Hungary, and Poland. Enormous economic, social, ecological, and ethnic problems present major obstacles to these changes, threatening them with failure, which would be accompanied by disastrous consequences for the entire world. The social justice and solidarity for which the socialist workers' movement has struggled are at stake. Socialism must rediscover its intended, democratic form if it is not to be lost to history. It cannot be allowed to fail; this endangered species, called humanity, needs other options to save human coexistence than the

Soviet leader Mikhail Gorbachev (referred to as "Gorbi" on the red banner) initiated changes that emboldened the East German population to demand greater democratic participation. (AP Images.)

example set by Western consumer societies, the prosperity of which must be paid for by the rest of the world.

Government whitewashing cannot hide the political, economic, and ecological signs of the crisis of state socialism "GDR style." The SED [Socialist Unity Party] leadership has not shown any willingness to change. It seems to be speculating on the failure of reform in the Soviet Union. The important thing now is to participate in this process of democratization.

The political crisis of GDR state socialism became particularly apparent in the local elections of 7 May 1989. The doctrine of the "moral-political unity of party, state, and people," which was used to justify a power monopoly independent of elections, could be confirmed only as a result of election fraud. Between 10 percent and 20 percent of the population in major cities openly refused to vote for National Front [East Germany's ruling condition, dominated by the SED] candidates. This figure would certainly have been considerably higher had balloting been secret.

So many people are no longer represented by the National Front; they lack any political representation at all in society. The wish of many citizens for a more democratic relationship between state and society still cannot be discussed publicly. For this reason, we appeal to all people to join the

CITIZENS' MOVEMENT 'DEMOCRACY NOW.'

CHAPTER 2

Controversies Surrounding the Berlin Wall

VIEWPOINT 1

The Berlin Wall Symbolized Increased Cold War Tensions

Louis J. Halle

In the following selection, historian Louis J. Halle makes the case that the construction of the Berlin Wall was a symptom of rising tensions between the United States and the Soviet Union, the primary combatants in the Cold War. As of 1958, tensions had been reduced somewhat when both sides had agreed to stop the testing of nuclear weapons. But, as Halle notes, by the end of 1961, the year the Wall went up, the Soviet Union was again vividly demonstrating its nuclear capability.

Halle's focus is on the two superpowers' respective leaders: Nikita Khrushchev in the Soviet Union and U.S. President John F. Kennedy, who took office in January 1961. The author argues that Khrushchev wanted the western powers to leave Berlin and hoped, at first, to accomplish that goal through negotiation and then through intimidation. Kennedy's stiff responses to Soviet moves sped up the rate of migrations from East to West until

Photo on previous page: The Brandenburg Gate's location near the center of Berlin put it in proximity to the wall that would later divide the city. (AP Images.)

SOURCE. Louis J. Halle, *The Cold War as History*. New York: Harper Torchbooks, 1967.

Soviet leaders decided to build the Berlin Wall.

Louis Halle was an official in the U.S. Department of State in the early 1950s and served as a professor at the Graduate School of International Relations in Geneva, Switzerland.

At the beginning of the 1960's there were signs in the West that people were beginning to weary of the Cold War, and to ask what sense it made. In the late 1940's everyone had been alarmed at the thought of the Red Army, which had already marched so far, continuing on to the English Channel; but this was no longer a plausible fear. The hysterical anti-Communism that had gripped the American people and their Government at the beginning of the 1950's had largely spent itself by the beginning of the 1960's. A disposition to move in the direction of a reasonable peace on the basis of live-and-let-live was beginning to have faint manifestations in the United States, while in Britain there had long been a popular tendency to blame the American ally for the continuation of the Cold War. If this tendency was not more overtly marked at the beginning of the 1960's it was because of the wild behavior with which the head of the Russian Government was repeatedly alarming the world.

This was the evolving situation at the beginning of 1961, when the Eisenhower Administration was replaced by the fresh Administration of President [John F.] Kennedy.

A New President

'On the Presidential coat of arms,' the new President told the nation, 'the American eagle holds in his right talon the olive branch, while in his left is held a bundle of arrows. We intend to give equal attention to both.' By the 1960's the dominant disposition of the American people and of the Western governments was to be equally ready either for possibilities of ending the Cold War or, in the absence of such possibilities, for holding their own in it—to be at once conciliatory and armed, to talk softly but carry a big stick.

> The two rival leaders of the world . . . agreed to meet each other face-to-face.

It is evident, however, that [Soviet leader Nikita] Khrushchev's whole policy, and consequently his survival as ruler of [the Soviet Union], now depended on his driving the Western allies out of Berlin. One can well imagine the mounting doubts among his associates in the Kremlin about his leadership, countered by his insistence that his policy needed more time to achieve the success he was sure it would bring; and one can imagine a reluctant decision to let him have the time. By now he must have felt like a man who goes about his business with a gun at his back.

Khrushchev's hope appears to have been that he would succeed with the new Administration of President Kennedy where he had failed with the Eisenhower Administration, which had proved unexpectedly stiff. On these grounds he had bought time, holding the campaign against Berlin in abeyance [temporary suspension] until the new Administration should establish itself in office. The new Administration, less blatantly anti-Communist than its predecessor, and disposed to look for possibilities of accommodation by compromise, might find itself freer to retreat at Berlin. It might also prove more responsive to the clamor of idealistic intellectuals throughout the West, who tended to regard a firm stand at Berlin as the demonstration of a criminal willingness to let the world be destroyed by nuclear war.

Once the Kennedy Administration was installed, however, Khrushchev could not delay for much longer the resumption of the drive on Berlin. Both the external situation, in which East Germany was being drained of its population through the Berlin escape-route, and the

Soviet leader Nikita Khrushchev may have hoped for President John F. Kennedy (left) to be more politically pliant with complete communist control of Berlin than President Dwight D. Eisenhower when the two met in 1961. (AP Images.)

position in which he found himself at home required it. First, however, the possibilities of an amicable settlement with the new Administration had to be tested. Friendly words for President Kennedy, and friendly gestures toward the United States, flowed from Moscow and were reciprocated by expressions of peaceful intent from Washington. The two rival leaders of the world, neither yet sure what to expect of the other, then agreed to meet each other face-to-face in private.

A Tense Meeting

The meeting took place in Vienna on June 3 and 4. It must have been revealing for both men, but especially for Kennedy. Khrushchev, who presented the Russian position in writing (perhaps because his colleagues in Moscow had to be assured of what he presented), appears to have left no doubt that he was determined to end the *status quo* in Berlin, if not by agreement with the West then in defiance of the West. The President appears to have been taken aback by the expression of that determination, and to have left Vienna with the somber conviction that in the next few months the world was to face a danger of imminent disaster.

In confirmation of this, on June 15 Khrushchev delivered an address in Moscow at which, as in November 1958, he again issued an ultimatum to the West. Russia, he said, was prepared to go ahead on its own to conclude with East Germany the peace treaty by which any rights of access to Berlin that the West might have would be terminated. Then, if the West violated the frontiers of East Germany it would 'receive a due rebuff.' The conclusion of such a treaty, he said, could not be 'postponed any longer,' but 'must be attained this year.' . . .

> Each side had suffered a blow to its international prestige.

On July 8 Khrushchev announced that, because of Western intransigence, Russia was abandoning a hitherto projected reduction in its armed forces and was increasing its defense expenditures by over a third. On July 25 Kennedy called for a substantial build-up of NATO forces and an increase in the American Army. 'We do not want to fight,' he said, 'but we have fought before. . . . We cannot and will not permit the Communists to drive us out of Berlin, either gradually or by force.' Khrushchev responded in a speech of August 7 by accusing the United States of 'carrying out mobilization measures, threatening to unleash a war.' He said it might be necessary to increase the numerical strength of the Red Army on the western frontiers and call up the reserves. Continued stubbornness by the West, he implied, might turn Berlin into another

The Cold War

From the end of World War II in 1945 to the collapse of the Soviet Union in 1991, world history was dominated by a single event: the Cold War. The basic conflict was between two governmental systems. One was representative democracy and capitalist economics as could be seen in the United States, one of the world's two superpowers in the Cold War era. The other system was Soviet-style communism, in which the state and a single party controlled both government and the economy, generally in very harsh terms that were limiting to individual freedoms. Like the United States, the Soviet Union emerged from World War II as a global superpower. Despite moments of danger the Cold War remained a conflict of threats, gestures, and negotiation rather than a hot, shooting war. One reason was that both sides came to maintain massive arsenals of nuclear weapons whose destructive power was so great that few ever conceived of actually using it.

The Cold War was truly a global conflict that was sometimes played out in localized "proxy" wars like the Korean War of the early 1950s and the Vietnam War of the 1960s and 1970s. But its center stage was in Europe; only there were American and Soviet forces standing face to face and only there did affluent democratic nations share borders with poorer Communist ones. After the Berlin Wall fell in 1989 as part of the larger movement among Eastern European nations to reject communism, and when the Soviet Union itself dissolved in the early 1990s, the Cold War was therefore over. Communist regimes remain in place in China, North Korea, Vietnam, Laos, and Cuba, but their continued existence does not make for a continued Cold War.

Sarajevo [a city in which a small incident sparks a major war], and he spoke of what the Soviet Union could do to the United States and its allies in a third world war.

The international tension, reaching the proportions of a full crisis, now prompted increasing numbers of East Germans to flee through the last door still open to them, fearing that at any moment it would be shut forever. During the first six months of 1961 over 103,000 had made their escape. Then, suddenly, the door was indeed slammed shut, although not in a way that anyone had expected.

The Wall Goes Up

Under the terms of the relevant agreements, Berlin had been administered as one city, with free circulation throughout. Many who lived in the Soviet sector had their places of work in the Western sectors; members of the same family might be living some on one side and some on the other of the imaginary line that separated the area of Soviet administration from the areas of American or British or French administration. At 2:30 A.M. on August 13 [1961], however, the East Germans sealed off West Berlin, except for a few official crossing-points where individuals could pass in and out under official inspection, and during the night of August 17–18, [1961] they began, on a crash basis, the construction of a concrete wall, topped with barbed wire, to cut the city in two.

"Crisis was now being piled on crisis."

The Western allies would have been within their legal rights if they had forcibly interfered with the construction of this wall, and it seems improbable (in tranquil retrospect) that such interference would have led to war. The risk hardly seemed sound at the time, however, and in any case a sober intergovernmental decision to take it could not have been reached in the middle of one night. Weeks and months later, the failure to interfere would be a cause of bitterness in the hearts of those who knew the human suffering and the sense of outrage that the Berlin Wall had produced. A still later judgment, however, can hardly overlook the evidence that the Wall, by stopping the disastrous drainage of the East German population, at last enabled Moscow to live with the situation created for it by the presence of the Western allies in Berlin.

A New Era of Crisis

The immediate effect, nevertheless, was not to lessen but to heighten the crisis. Each side had suffered a blow to its international prestige, the West by allowing the Wall to be built, the Communists by providing such visible evidence of the captivity in which their populations were held. For the moment, then, each side was impelled to strike heroic attitudes. Vice President Lyndon Johnson flew from Washington to Berlin, to be followed by General Lucius Clay, the symbol of the resistance to the 1948 blockade, and a reinforcement of 1,500 American soldiers. Moscow accused the West of misusing the air-corridors to Berlin by flying in West German 'revanchists, extremists, saboteurs, and spies.' Emergency military preparations were made on both sides.

Crisis was now being piled on crisis. Again people all over the world stopped sleeping. Again the Western governments had to resist the pressure of articulate intellectuals who were morally outraged by the apparent willingness of the politicians to risk a third world war rather than make peace with Moscow on its terms. Round-about Trafalgar Square in London marched little groups of men and women in single file, the flame of righteousness in their eyes, bearing placards that demanded unilateral nuclear disarmament now.

Since the beginning of November 1958, the United States, Britain, and Russia, by tacit [unspoken] agreement, had discontinued the nuclear test explosions that had been poisoning the atmosphere of the whole northern hemisphere and thereby endangering the future of mankind. Now, on August 21 [1961], Moscow announced that, because the United States and its allies were threatening to unleash a war 'as a counter-measure to the conclusion of a peace treaty with the German Democratic Republic,' its obligation to 'cool the hotheads in the capitals of certain NATO powers' required it to resume nuclear testing. Beginning the following day, the Russians successively produced some fifty nuclear explosions, culminating in one of over 50 megatons on October 30 [1961], that were designed to intimidate a Western world which, however frightened it might be, was still standing firm.

VIEWPOINT 2

The Berlin Wall Helped to Lessen Cold War Conflict

Tony Judt

The status of Berlin was a source of uncertainty in Cold War diplomacy beginning with the very onset of the Cold War in the late 1940s. In the following selection, historian Tony Judt argues that the construction of the Berlin Wall actually helped to reduce this uncertainty and therefore the importance of Berlin as a Cold War flashpoint.

During the Berlin blockade and airlift of 1948–1949 and again in the late 1950s and early 1960s, disagreements over Berlin presented the chance of the Cold War becoming a hot, shooting war, even the beginning of a World War III. In addition, Soviet and East German leaders resented the fact that West Berlin made possible a flood of migrants from East to West and wanted the strange situation of a city divided by politics but nothing else to be settled. Their only choices were to force the West out of Berlin, which proved impossible, or to build the

---

SOURCE. Tony Judt, *Postwar: A History of Europe Since 1945*. New York: Penguin Books, 2006.

Berlin Wall. Judt suggests that American politicians, despite commitments to defend West Berlin and West Germany with military force if necessary, were content enough that the wall had been built. Its presence simply made Berlin, and disputes over it, more stable.

British historian Tony Judt is a professor of European studies at New York University and a fellow of the American Academy of Arts and Sciences.

The first move in the 'Berlin crisis' came on November 10th 1958, when [Soviet Premier Nikita] Khrushchev made a public speech in Moscow, addressed to the Western powers:

> The imperialists have turned the German question into an abiding source of international tension. The ruling circles of Western Germany are doing everything to whip up military passions against the German Democratic Republic. . . . Speeches by [West German] Chancellor Adenauer and Defense Minister Strauss, the atomic arming of the Bundeswehr [West Germany] and various military exercises all speak of a definite trend in the policy of the ruling circles of West Germany. . . . The time has obviously arrived for the signatories of the Potsdam Agreement [of 1945] to give up the remnants of the occupation regime in Berlin and thereby make it possible to create a normal situation in the capital of the German Democratic Republic [GDR]. The Soviet Union, for its part, would hand over to the sovereign German Democratic Republic the functions in Berlin that are still exercised by Soviet agencies.

The ostensible objective of Khrushchev's offensive, which took on a greater urgency when the Soviet leader demanded two weeks later that the West make up its mind to withdraw from Berlin within six months, was to get the Americans to abandon Berlin and allow it to become a 'free city'. If they did so, the credibility

> From November 1958 through the summer of 1961 the crisis over Berlin simmered.

of their general commitment to the defense of Western Europe would be seriously dented, and neutralist, anti-nuclear sentiment in West Germany and elsewhere would probably grow. But even if the Western powers insisted on staying put in Berlin, the USSR might be able to exchange its consent to this for a firm Western commitment to deny Bonn [West Germany] any nuclear weapons.

When Western leaders refused any concessions over Berlin, claiming that the Soviet Union itself had broken its Potsdam undertakings [the original 1945 agreement separating Berlin into sectors] by integrating East Berlin fully into the government and institutions of the East German state before any final Treaty had been agreed, Khrushchev tried again. Following an unsuccessful series of foreign ministers' discussions in Geneva in the summer of 1959, he repeated his demands, first in 1960 and then again in June 1961. The Western military presence in Berlin must end. Otherwise the Soviet Union would unilaterally withdraw from Berlin, conclude a separate Peace Treaty with the GDR and leave the West to negotiate the fate of its zones of occupation with an independent East German state. From November 1958 through the summer of 1961 the crisis over Berlin simmered, diplomatic nerves frayed and the exodus of East Germans grew to a flood.

A Tense Summit Meeting

Khrushchev's June 1961 ultimatum was delivered at a summit meeting with John F. Kennedy, the new American President, held in Vienna. The last such summit meeting, between Khrushchev and Eisenhower in May 1960, had been abandoned when the Soviets shot down US Air Force pilot Gary Powers in his U2 plane and the Americans reluctantly conceded that they had

Dean Rusk, President Kennedy's secretary of state, believed the wall "would make a Berlin settlement [with the Soviet Union] easier." (**AP Images.**)

indeed been conducting high-altitude espionage (having first denied all knowledge of the matter). In his talks with Kennedy, Khrushchev threatened to 'liquidate' Western rights in Berlin if there was no settlement there by the end of the year.

In public Kennedy, like Eisenhower before him, took a hard line, insisting that the West would never abandon its commitments. Washington was standing by its rights under the Potsdam accords and increasing the national defense budget specifically to buttress the US military presence in Germany. But off the record the US was much more accommodating. The Americans—unlike their West German clients—accepted the reality of an East German state, and understood Soviet anxiety over the aggressive tone of recent speeches by Adenauer and, especially, his Defense Minister Franz Josef Strauss. Something had to be done to move the German situation forward—as Eisenhower said to [British Prime Minister Harold] Macmillan on March 28th 1960, the West couldn't 'really afford to stand on a dime for the next fifty years.' In a similar spirit, Kennedy assured Khrushchev at Vienna that the United States did not 'wish to act in a way that would deprive the Soviet Union of its ties in Eastern Europe': a veiled acknowledgement that what the Russians had, they could hold, including the eastern zone of Germany and the former German territories now in Poland, Czechoslovakia and the Soviet Union.

Shortly after Kennedy returned to Washington, the East German authorities began imposing travel restrictions on would-be emigrants. In direct response, the US President publicly re-asserted the Western commitment to *West* Berlin—thereby implicitly conceding that the city's eastern half was in the Soviet sphere of influence. The rate of exodus through Berlin grew faster than ever: 30,415 people left for the West in July; by the first week of August 1961 a further 21,828 had followed, half of them under twenty-five years of age. At this rate the German Democratic Republic would soon be empty.

Dividing a City

Khrushchev's response was to cut the Gordian knot [metaphor for complex problem] of Berlin. After the Allied foreign ministers, meeting in Paris on August 6th, rejected yet another Soviet note threatening a separate Peace Treaty with the GDR if a settlement was not reached, Moscow authorized the East Germans to draw

> A wall across Berlin was a far better outcome than a war.

a line, literally, separating the two sides once and for all. On August 19th 1961 the East Berlin authorities set soldiers and workmen to the task of building a partition across the city. Within three days a rough wall had been erected, sufficient to foreclose casual movement between the two halves of Berlin. Over the ensuing weeks it was raised and strengthened. Searchlights, barbed wire and guard posts were added; the doors and windows of buildings abutting the wall were first blocked off, and then bricked up. Streets and squares were cut in half and all communications across the divided city were subjected to close policing or else broken off altogether. Berlin had its Wall.

Officially the West was horrified. For three days in October 1961 Soviet and American tanks confronted one another across the checkpoint separating their respective zones—one of the last remaining links between them—as the East German authorities tested the Western powers' willingness to affirm and assert their continuing right of access to the eastern zone in keeping with the original Four-Power Agreement. Faced with the intransigence of the local American military commander—who refused to recognize any *East German* right to impede Allied movements—the Soviets reluctantly granted the point; for the next thirty years all four occupying powers remained in place, although both sides conceded *de facto* administration of their respective zones of control to the local German authorities.

Behind the scenes many Western leaders were secretly relieved at the appearance of the Wall. For three years Berlin had threatened to be the flashpoint for an international confrontation, just as it had been in 1948. Kennedy and other Western leaders privately agreed that a wall across Berlin was a far better outcome than a war—whatever was said in public, few Western politicians could seriously imagine asking their soldiers to 'die for Berlin.' As Dean Rusk (Kennedy's Secretary of State) quietly observed, the Wall had its uses: 'the probability is that in realistic terms it would make a Berlin settlement easier'.

The outcome of the Berlin crisis showed that the two Great Powers had more in common than they sometimes appreciated. If Moscow undertook not to raise again the question of Allied status in Berlin, Washington would accept the reality of East German government there and would resist West German pressure for nuclear weapons. Both sides had an interest in stability in central Europe; but more to the point, the US and the USSR were both tired of responding to the demands and complaints of their respective German clients. The first decade of the Cold War had given German politicians on either side of the divide unparalleled leverage over their patrons in Washington and Moscow. Afraid of losing credibility with 'their' Germans, the Great Powers had allowed Adenauer and [East German leader Walter] Ulbricht to blackmail them into 'hanging tough'.

A New Cold War Understanding

Moscow, which . . . had never set out to establish a client state in the eastern zone of occupied Germany, but had settled for it as a second best, devoted inordinate effort to shoring up a weak and unloved Communist regime in Berlin. The East German Communists in their turn were always half-afraid that their Soviet patrons would sell them out. The Wall thus offered them some reassurance, although they were disappointed by Khrushchev's refusal to keep pressing for a Peace Treaty once the barrier had gone up. As for Bonn, the longstanding fear there was that the 'Amis' (Americans) would just get up and walk away. Washington had always bent over backwards to reassure Bonn that it had America's unswerving support, but after the Wall went up and the Americans conspicuously acquiesced, West German anxiety only increased. Hence the reiterated post-Wall promises from Washington that the US would never quit their zone—the background to Kennedy's famous 'Ich bin ein Berliner' (*sic*) ["I am a Berliner"] declaration in June 1963. With 250,000 troops in Europe by 1963, the Americans like the Russians were clearly there for the duration.

The Wall ended Berlin's career as the crisis zone of world and European affairs. Although it took ten years to reach formal agreement on issues of access, after November 1961 Berlin ceased to matter and West Berlin began its steady descent into political irrelevance.

VIEWPOINT 3

East Germany Contends That Greater Border Controls Are Necessary

Council of Ministers, German Democratic Republic (East Germany)

Construction of the Berlin Wall began on August 13, 1961. That same day the Warsaw Pact alliance, which consisted of the Soviet Union and its Communist satellite states in Eastern Europe, issued a public statement condemning what it saw as the West's military and territorial aggression with regard to Berlin and East Germany. The East German government issued a statement a day earlier, which is the selection below.

In addition to condemning the West's alleged militarism, which the East German officials charged was a return to the fascism of the World War II era, the declaration notes that the government needs to take certain measures to "secure peace." These were to include, most notably, increased border restric-

---

SOURCE. *Uniting Germany: Documents and Debates, 1944–1993.* Providence, RI: Berghahn Books, 1994.

tions. The declaration does not mention in any direct way the building of a wall across the capital city.

On the basis of the declaration of the Warsaw Pact member states and the Volkskammer [People's Chamber, or East Germany's governing body] resolution, the Council of Ministers of the GDR [German Democratic Republic, or East Germany] has resolved:

In the interest of peace, the actions of West German revanchists [who want to restore the old borders] and militarists need to be stopped and, by means of a German peace treaty, the way must be paved for peace and the rebirth of Germany as a peace-loving, anti-imperialist, neutral state. The standpoint of the [West German] government in Bonn—that World War II has not yet ended—is tantamount to a call for a license for militaristic provocation and civil war measures. Such imperialistic policy disguised as anti-communism represents a continuation of the aggressive goals of fascist German imperialism at the time of the Third Reich. The defeat of Hitlerian Germany in World War II has led the Bonn government to give the criminal politics of German monopoly capitalism and its Hitler generals another try by renouncing the policy of a German nation-state and transforming West Germany into a NATO [North Atlantic Treaty Organization] state, a satellite of the United States.

> Borders to West Berlin will be sufficiently guarded . . . to prevent subversive activities from the West.

This new threat to the German and European peoples through German militarism could become an acute danger, since the West German Federal Republic and the front city of West Berlin have continually violated the basic stipulations of the Potsdam Agreement [of 1945] that call for eradication of militarism and Nazism.

THE BERLIN WALL

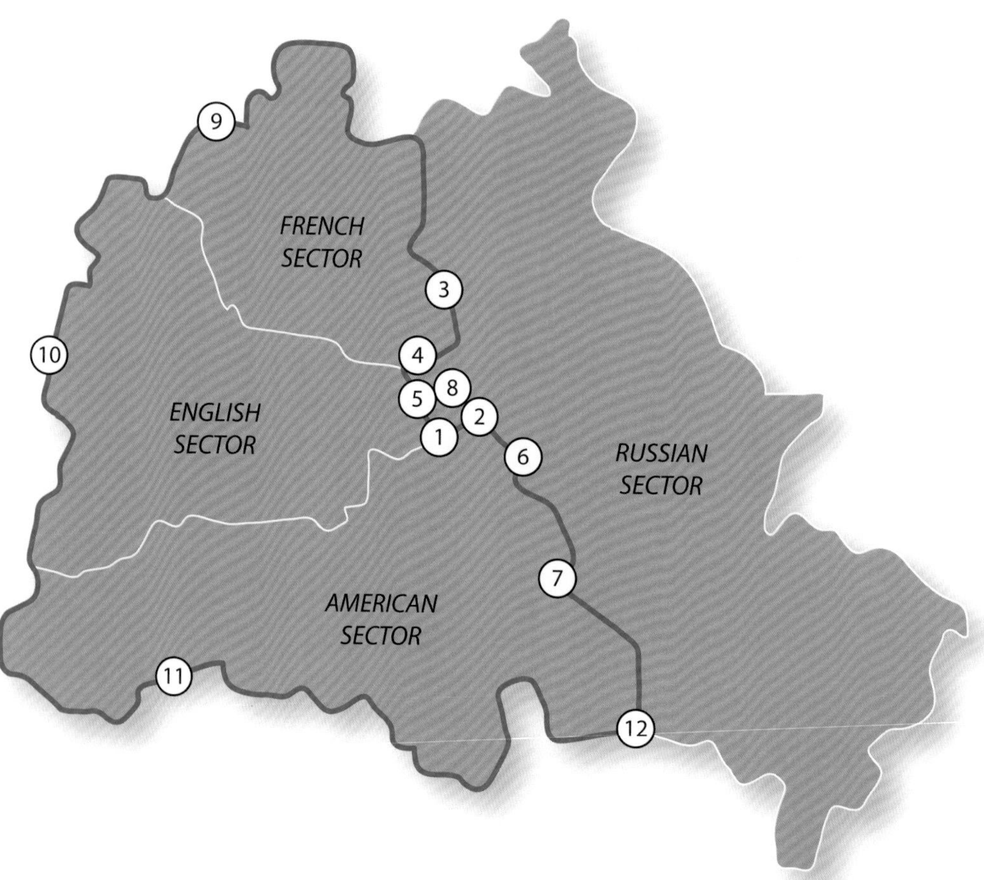

The Crossing Points between West and East Berlin	The Crossing Points between West Berlin and GDR
1 Checkpoint Charlie	9 Heiligensee/Stolpe
2 Heinrich-Heine-Strasse	10 Staaken
3 Bornholmer Strasse	11 Dreilinden/Drewitz
4 Chausseestrasse	12 Waltersdorfer Chaussee
5 Invalidenstrasse	
6 Oberbaumbrücke	Berlin Wall
7 Sannenallee	
8 Friedrichstrasse Station	

Taken from: German Missions in the United States, www.germany.info.

Revanchism has intensified in West Germany, with increasing territorial claims against the GDR and neighboring states. This sentiment is closely tied to accelerated rearmament and acquisition of nuclear weaponry by the West German army. The Adenauer administration [in Bonn] is making systematic preparations for civil war against the GDR. Citizens of the GDR who visit West Germany are increasingly subject to terrorist persecution. West German and West Berlin espionage headquarters are systematically soliciting citizens of the GDR and organizing the smuggling of human beings.

As formulated in official government documents and the declaration of principles of the CDU/CSU [West Germany's Christian Democratic Union and Christian Social Union] party leadership, the goal of this aggressive policy and these disruptive activities is to incorporate all of Germany into NATO, the western military bloc, and extend the militaristic rule of the Federal Republic onto the territory of the GDR. West German militarists wish to use all kinds of deceptive maneuvers, such as "free elections," in order to expand their military basis first as far as the Oder River [the GDR's eastern border] and then begin the great war.

West German revanchists and militarists are abusing the peaceful policies of the USSR and Warsaw Pact states in regard to the German question. Their intentions are to use hostile agitation, solicitation, and diversionary maneuvers to harm not only the GDR but other socialist states as well.

For all these reasons, the Council of Ministers of the GDR, in accordance with the resolution by the Political Advisory Committee of the states of the Warsaw Pact, is instituting the following measures to secure peace in Europe and protect the GDR, and in the interest of ensuring the security of states in the socialist camp:

To stop hostile activities by revanchist and militaristic forces in West Germany and West Berlin, a border con-

According to East German officials, the Western powers—France, Great Britain, and the United States—sought to incorporate all of Germany into their military bloc. (**Keenpress/Hulton Archive/Getty Images.**)

trol will be introduced at the borders to the GDR, including the border with western sectors of Greater Berlin, as is common on the borders of sovereign states. Borders to West Berlin will be sufficiently guarded and effectively controlled in order to prevent subversive activities from the West. Citizens of the GDR will require a special permit to cross these borders. Until West Berlin is transformed into a demilitarized, neutral, free city, residents of the capital of the GDR will require a special certificate to cross the border into West Berlin. Peaceful citizens of West Berlin are permitted to visit the capital of the GDR (democratic Berlin) upon presentation of a West Berlin identity card. Revanchist politicians and agents of West German militarism are not permitted to enter the capital of the GDR (democratic Berlin). For citizens of the West German Federal Republic wishing to visit democratic Berlin, previous control regulations remain in effect.

Entry by citizens of other states to the capital of the GDR will not be affected by these regulations.

For travel by citizens of West Berlin via routes through the GDR to other states, previous regulations remain in effect.

Transit traffic between West Germany and West Berlin through the GDR will not be affected by this resolution.

The Minister of the Interior, the Minister for Transport, and the Mayor of Greater Berlin are called upon to enact any measures necessary for the implementation of this resolution.

This resolution on measures to secure peace, protect the GDR, in particular the capital city of Berlin, and assure the security of other socialist states will remain in effect until conclusion of a German peace treaty.

VIEWPOINT 4

All Free People Are Berliners

John F. Kennedy

In that part of the city where once stood West Berlin's city hall, an open area is known as John F. Kennedy Square. It was there, on June 26, 1963, that President Kennedy made one of his most famous speeches on foreign policy, with 120,000 West Berliners in attendance. That speech appears here.

Since the beginning of the construction of the Berlin Wall in 1961, Kennedy had reiterated American support for maintaining the free status of West Berlin. But it was his 1963 visit to the city, part of a tour of five European countries, that is most often remembered. In his speech, Kennedy noted that West Berlin remained a "defended island of freedom" and as such a blow against communism everywhere. Speaking the German phrase twice, Kennedy also claimed that to say, "I am a Berliner" was the "proudest boast." The event ended with the bell of West Berlin's city hall tolling, over a silent crowd, in remembrance of the people of East Germany.

SOURCE. John F. Kennedy, "Speech on West Berlin," in www.historicaldocuments.com, June 26, 1963.

> I know of no town, no city, that has been besieged for 18 years that still lives with the vitality and the force, and the hope and the determination of the city of West Berlin.

I am proud to come to this city as the guest of your distinguished Mayor [Willy Brandt], who has symbolized throughout the world the fighting spirit of West Berlin. And I am proud to visit the Federal Republic with your distinguished Chancellor who for so many years has committed Germany to democracy and freedom and progress, and to come here in the company of my fellow American, General [Lucius] Clay, who has been in this city during its great moments of crisis and will come again if ever needed. Two thousand years ago the proudest boast was "*civis Romanus sum* [I am a citizen of Rome]." Today, in the world of freedom, the proudest boast is "*Ich bin ein Berliner* [I am a Berliner]." I appreciate my interpreter translating my German!

There are many people in the world who really don't understand, or say they don't, what is the great issue between the free world and the Communist world. Let them come to Berlin. There are some who say that communism is the wave of the future. Let them come to Berlin. And there are some who say in Europe and elsewhere we can work with the Communists. Let them come to Berlin. And there are even a few who say that it is true that communism is an evil system, but it permits us to make economic progress. *Lass' sie nach Berlin kommen* [Let them come to Berlin]. Let them come to Berlin.

Freedom has many difficulties and democracy is not perfect, but we have never had to put a wall up to keep our people in, to prevent them from leaving us. I want to say, on behalf of my countrymen, who live many miles away on the other side of the Atlantic, who are far distant from you, that they take the greatest pride that they have been able to share with you, even from a distance,

During his speech to Berliners on June 26, 1963, U.S. President John F. Kennedy urged his audience to look forward to their city's reunification. **(Art Rickerby/Time Life Pictures/Getty Images.)**

the story of the last 18 years. I know of no town, no city, that has been besieged for 18 years that still lives with the vitality and the force, and the hope and the determination of the city of West Berlin. While the wall is the most obvious and vivid demonstration of the failures of the Communist system, for all the world to see, we take no satisfaction in it, for it is, as your Mayor has said, an offense not only against history but an offense against humanity, separating families, dividing husbands and wives and brothers and sisters, and dividing a people who wish to be joined together.

What is true of this city is true of Germany—real, lasting peace in Europe can never be assured as long as one German out of four is denied the elementary right of free men, and that is to make a free choice. In 18 years of peace and good faith, this generation of Germans has earned the right to be free, including the right to unite

Did Kennedy Misspeak?

Shortly before he was scheduled to make a major Cold War speech in West Berlin in June 1963, President John F. Kennedy decided to include the phrase, "I am a Berliner," signifying both his personal identification with, and American support for, the residents of a city recently divided by a wall. He also decided to speak the phrase in German and had it translated by an interpreter. When Kennedy said, before thousands of West Berliners, that "as a free man, I take pride in the words, "*Ich bin ein Berliner*," the crowd cheered loudly and evidently had no trouble understanding what he meant.

Nonetheless, some writers and commentators have suggested that Kennedy made a humorous grammatical error: instead of saying, "I am a Berliner," the president had said, "I am a jelly donut." Indeed, in many parts of Germany a particular kind of pastry with a fruit filling is known as a Berliner. What Kennedy should have said, some claim, is "*Ich bin Berliner*," the proper formulation for claiming citizenship or residency, not "*Ich bin ein Berliner*."

The jelly donut story has taken on a life of its own but, in truth, Kennedy spoke correctly. The formulation "*Ich bin Berliner*" is common, familiar language for actual residents of the city but to say "*Ich bin ein Berliner*" would be perfectly correct in more formal German or for someone who was speaking figuratively. Meanwhile, the fruit-filled pastry under question, while popular in Berlin, is known there as a "pfannkuchen."

their families and their nation in lasting peace, with good will to all people. You live in a defended island of freedom, but your life is part of the main. So let me ask you as I close, to lift your eyes beyond the dangers of today, to the hopes of tomorrow, beyond the freedom merely of this city of Berlin, or your country of Germany, to the advance of freedom everywhere, beyond the wall to the day of peace with justice, beyond yourselves and ourselves to all mankind.

Freedom is indivisible, and when one man is enslaved, all are not free. When all are free, then we can look forward to that day when this city will be joined as one and this country and this great continent of Europe in a peaceful and hopeful globe. When that day finally comes, as it will, the people of West Berlin can take sober satisfaction in the fact that they were in the front lines for almost two decades.

All free men, wherever they may live, are citizens of Berlin, and, therefore, as a free man, I take pride in the words "*Ich bin ein Berliner*."

VIEWPOINT 5

The Berlin Wall Ensures a Continued Relationship Between West Berlin and the United States

Eleanor Lansing Dulles

In the following selection, diplomat and author Eleanor Lansing Dulles argues that the continued free status of West Berlin was an essential priority for American policy makers once the Berlin Wall was in place. Among the reasons, she asserts, was that Soviet and other Communist leaders could not be trusted to hold to their agreements. But, even more importantly, the very vulnerability of the city meant that leaders had to pay special attention to it.

West Berlin lay deep inside the borders of Communist East Germany. Its entrances were guarded by fortifications, barbed

---

SOURCE. Eleanor Lansing Dulles, *Berlin: The Wall is Not Forever*. Chapel Hill, NC: University of North Carolina Press, 1967.

wire, and after 1961, a long concrete wall. It could be reached from the outside by rail, road, air, or barge (on rivers and canals) but access was controlled by international agreements and was not, as Dulles argues, "normal" or free. West Berlin was not an easy city to protect, Dulles asserts, but American leaders had made a commitment to do so, and the people of West Berlin trusted that commitment.

Eleanor Lansing Dulles, whose family included former secretaries of state and a director of the Central Intelligence Agency, worked for the U.S. Department of State for 20 years and later taught at Duke and Georgetown universities.

The erection of the Wall, and the hesitation of the Western Powers to exert their legal rights on this and other occasions, indicates in dramatic fashion the vulnerable position of Berlin in this atomic age. The fact that there is no easy way to protect the freedom of the city, when the United States is endeavoring to avoid a clash and at the same time protect our vital interests there and elsewhere, augments the difficulties of the day-to-day protection of the city. In some instances, the issue seems too slight to invoke the protective shield of NATO [North Atlantic Treaty Organization, the West's main military and diplomatic alliance] or to use the armed might of Western nations. The imbalance of the significance of a delay of traffic on the autobahn [German highway] and the threat of world war, shock many to inaction in a situation where swift and decisive response would be the best answer to Communist harassment. Varied geographic, economic, political, and psychological elements of the situation plague those who would protect the city [Berlin].

> There are few cities more tortured, more beset with difficulties, and, from a purely strategic point of view, more vulnerable.

How does this city, with its wall of division and its narrow corridors to the outside world, differ from other cities of the world? One could stay

Despite its division, Berlin remained a populous cultural hub. (Sahm Doherty/ Time Life Pictures/Getty Images.)

there a month, even a year, and if not politically minded, could think of it much as one would think of any city. In spite of both economic and political strength, the city is vulnerable from many points of view.

A Vital and Active City

Berlin has more cultural life than today's Washington, more theaters, concerts, art students—a new Art Academy and interesting churches and educational institutions—and a more vital air. It will soon have one of the best hospitals in the world. Many conference halls, museums, and sports arenas are available. It has an atomic research reactor. Its shopping centers are attractive. Its restaurants are good. Its night clubs are gay. Some 100,000 to 200,000 tourists visit the city every month.

This city of two and a quarter million is one of the major industrial centers of the world. Few metropolitan areas, none if the comparison is with the central city areas, not taking the suburbs into account, produce as much in value as Berlin. This is a city without a hinterland. For years the barbed wire has been strong around the outer limits of the city. It is a workshop that must get all its raw materials from miles away, usually 150 to 200 miles or farther. It is a city dependent on three main roads and three air corridors for its material and psychological support. It is a city surrounded by hostility. It is a living center that powerful forces are determined to destroy.

It is recognized that in the developed countries there are few cities more tortured, more beset with difficulties, and, from a purely strategic point of view, more vulnerable. Here, where the shooting war stopped more than twenty years ago, there is a city still occupied, still paying millions of dollars in occupation costs to the visitors, still without full constitutional and legal rights. Here is one of the main battlegrounds of the cold war. A place where innocent men, wishing to visit friends, relatives, children, are shot on sight—by men of the same nationality, in broad daylight—because they step into a cleared strip of the city's streets to cross an unlawful political boundary, set by hate and force. Here is perhaps the most critical dilemma of the free world, and one of the most puzzling and frustrating problems for the Communist world. Here the aggressive Soviet march was halted and remains stalled for the foreseeable future.

The people of Berlin are as confident as an expert on the tight wire. They, like such a man, expect the sense of balance to keep them suspended in their precarious position with no disaster for the time they need to reach security. They think they can withstand the disturbing efforts of Communist bullies to shake their poise. They know that in a split second all can be lost. They depend on the Western Allies for the support that is the very essence of their safety.

> 'Surely the Americans . . . will not desert us.'

Dependent on an American Presence

They think we will stand by them because we have promised and because we have stood by them in the past. They are accustomed to our commitment; they like to see our soldiers marching on their streets on the Fourth of July with fifty state flags waving. The military reviews are attended by large crowds. They are happy when our tanks rumble down Clay-Allee [a Berlin street named for an American general] on a Saturday morning. They like our visitors, they are tolerant of American ways, and they think of the GI's as friends and protectors.

The more sophisticated are sure that the entire German position, as it now exists, is an essential element of NATO. They conclude that if the keystone of Berlin is pulled out of the structure, and if the Americans acquiesce in weakness, the credibility of the alliance will crumble. In spite of their casual behavior, there is always beneath the surface of their faith a gnawing fear that some day the whole intricate structure will seem to be too troublesome for the United States.

In this special psychological and political sensitivity is rooted the unique situation of a city which seems in most respects so normal. Not even the Wall is so great a threat to the future of Berlin as would be the misstatement of a President in Washington, an unwitting declaration in Congress, or the inept remark of a responsible official. In fact, any act or word that might throw doubt on the continued maintenance of the Western position could have serious results. The life of the city hangs on a phrase, on a promise.

It is easy to hypothesize a series of events which would lead to panic. It almost happened in 1948, in 1958, in 1961. The consequences of disillusion in Berlin and Bonn [the capital of West Germany] would mean an outflow of people, a flight of funds, a blow to industry, a collapse of the standard of living, a sudden increase in unemployment, a loss of morale, a downfall of the whole brilliant structure. As of today, the Berliners shrug their shoulders. We can hear them say again, as they have for a dozen years, "We have stood harassment, we have faced danger, we have laughed at threats, we have built and traded, improved our plants and increased productivity. We have drunk and danced and sung. We have pride and expectations for the future. Surely the Americans who sent their boys to fly the [1948] airlift, who gave us millions, who have waited in convoys at the barriers, who have lived with us for twenty years—surely they will not desert us."

The reasons for this sensitivity and this trust are obvious. They lie in the geography of Berlin, in the zig and zag of Communist action, sometimes in the fluctuating Allied reactions.

Soviet Inconsistencies

The overwhelming importance of the American commitment to defend Berlin along with that of the French, the British, and the other NATO Allies, results not from the failure to make proper agreements about the city, but in the refusal of the Soviets to honor the letter or the spirit of the agreements that have been made from the time of the European Advisory Committee in 1944, Yalta in 1945, the Paris meeting of 1949, and the Geneva summit statement of 1955. In all of these, the method of handling Germany—and the goal for a postwar Germany, implied or stated—was that there should be economic unification of the area, leaving for later decisions on the Eastern territories, with normal traffic in and out of Berlin. The fact that traffic has not been completely normal since the 1945 surrender and that it became increasingly circumscribed over the years was a matter that was politically disregarded at times. In other times, as during the Blockade or periods of intense harassment, it brought the world close to atomic war.

The statesmen on both sides of the Iron Curtain, in spite of Soviet deviations, recognize the interconnections of the series of treaties and arrangements. These commitments are firm and not subject to unilateral modification.

It is because the Soviets have a duality of views and have broken their own agreements that there is no basis for the citizens of Berlin to put their faith in future promises of the Kremlin. They are convinced that their lives and destinies cannot be made secure by a treaty with no visible American support. The memories of the old men and the experience of the young have joined their security with the American soldier. The stars and stripes mean more to them than diplomatic protocols. They have concluded that Berlin represents for America a vital interest.

VIEWPOINT 6

"Mr. Gorbachev, Tear Down This Wall!"

Ronald Reagan

In June 1987, U.S. President Ronald Reagan traveled to West Berlin. There, like his predecessor John F. Kennedy, he made a speech that became an essential piece of Cold War history. Parts of that speech are excerpted as the following selection.

Elected first in 1980, Reagan had at first taken a harsh stand toward the Soviet Union and its presence in places like East Germany and Berlin. But after 1985, and in his second term, Reagan grew interested in the reforms proposed by the new Soviet leader Mikhail Gorbachev. He remained cautious but was hopeful that Gorbachev's reforms might result in greater freedom for people living in Communist nations in Europe. In his speech, he noted that West Berliners had risen from the destruction of World War II to provide a vivid example of such freedoms. Reagan urged Gorbachev to demonstrate his sincerity in extending those freedoms and to "tear down this wall" separating the city, visible from the Brandenburg Gate, the Berlin landmark where Reagan made his speech.

SOURCE. Ronald Reagan, "Remarks at the Brandenburg Gate," www.reaganlibrary.com, June 12, 1987. Reproduced by permission.

Twenty-four years ago, President John F. Kennedy visited Berlin, speaking to the people of this city and the world at the City Hall. Well, since then two other presidents have come, each in his turn, to Berlin. And today I, myself, make my second visit to your city.

We come to Berlin, we American presidents, because it's our duty to speak, in this place, of freedom. But I must confess, we're drawn here by other things as well: by the feeling of history in this city, more than 500 years older than our own nation; by the beauty of the Grunewald and the Tiergarten; most of all, by your courage and determination. Perhaps the composer Paul Lincke understood something about American presidents. You see, like so many presidents before me, I come here today because wherever I go, whatever I do: *Ich hab noch einen Koffer in Berlin.* [I still have a suitcase in Berlin.]

> As long as this scar of a wall is permitted to stand, it is not the German question alone that remains open, but the question of freedom for all mankind.

Our gathering today is being broadcast throughout Western Europe and North America. I understand that it is being seen and heard as well in the East. To those listening throughout Eastern Europe, a special word: Although I cannot be with you, I address my remarks to you just as surely as to those standing here before me. For I join you, as I join your fellow countrymen in the West, in this firm, this unalterable belief: *Es gibt nur ein Berlin.* [There is only one Berlin.]

Behind me stands a wall that encircles the free sectors of this city, part of a vast system of barriers that divides the entire continent of Europe. From the Baltic, south, those barriers cut across Germany in a gash of barbed wire, concrete, dog runs, and guard towers. Farther south, there may be no visible, no obvious wall. But there remain armed guards and checkpoints all the same—still a restriction on the right to travel, still an instrument to impose upon ordinary men and women the will of a totalitarian state. Yet it is here in Berlin where the wall emerges most clearly; here, cutting across your city, where the news photo and the television screen have imprinted this brutal division of a continent upon the mind of the world. Standing before the Brandenburg Gate, every man is a German, separated from his fellow men. Every man is a Berliner, forced to look upon a scar.

[West German] President von Weizsacker has said, "The German question is open as long as the Brandenburg Gate is closed." Today I say: As long as the gate is closed, as long as this scar of a wall is permitted to stand, it is not the German question alone that remains open, but the question of freedom for all mankind. Yet I do not come here to lament. For I find in Berlin a message of hope, even in the shadow of this wall, a message of triumph.

West Germany's Revival

In this season of spring, in 1945, the people of Berlin emerged from their air-raid shelters to find devastation. Thousands of miles away, the people of the United States reached out to help. And in 1947 Secretary of State—as you've been told—George Marshall announced the creation of what would become known as the Marshall Plan [American economic aid to Germany and other countries]. Speaking precisely 40 years ago this month, he said: "Our policy is directed not against any country or doctrine, but against hunger, poverty, desperation, and chaos."

In the Reichstag a few moments ago, I saw a display commemorating this 40th anniversary of the Marshall Plan. I was struck by the sign on a burnt-out, gutted structure that was being rebuilt. I understand that Berliners of my own generation can remember seeing signs like it dotted throughout the western sectors of the city. The sign read simply: "The Marshall Plan is helping here to strengthen the free world." A strong, free world in the West, that dream became real. Japan rose from ruin to become an economic giant. Italy, France, Belgium—virtually every nation in Western Europe saw political and economic rebirth; the European community was founded.

In West Germany and here in Berlin, there took place an economic miracle, the *Wirtschaftswunder*. Adenauer, Erhard, Reuter [earlier West German leaders], and other leaders understood the practical importance of liberty—that just as truth can flourish only when the journalist is given freedom of speech, so prosperity can come about only when the farmer and businessman enjoy economic freedom. The German leaders reduced tariffs, expanded free trade, lowered taxes. From 1950 to 1960 alone, the standard of living in West Germany and Berlin doubled.

Where four decades ago there was rubble, today in West Berlin there is the greatest industrial output of any city in Germany—busy office blocks, fine homes and apartments, proud avenues, and the spreading lawns of parkland. Where a city's culture seemed to have been destroyed, today there are two great universities, orchestras and an opera, countless theaters, and museums. Where there was want, today there's abundance—food, clothing, automobiles—the wonderful goods of the Ku'damm. From devastation, from utter ruin, you Berliners have, in freedom, rebuilt a city that once again ranks as one of the greatest on earth. The Soviets may have had other plans. But my friends, there were a few things the Soviets didn't count on—*Berliner Herz, Berliner Humor, ja, und Berliner Schnauze* [Berliner heart, Berliner humor, yes, and a Berliner Schnauze].

In the 1950s, [then-Soviet leader Nikita] Khrushchev predicted: "We

> "And now the Soviets themselves may . . . be coming to understand the importance of freedom."

Many credit U.S. President Ronald Reagan's speech at the Brandenburg Gate on June 12, 1987, with speeding the fall of the Berlin Wall. **(Dirck Halstead/ Getty Images.)**

will bury you." But in the West today, we see a free world that has achieved a level of prosperity and well-being unprecedented in all human history. In the Communist world, we see failure, technological backwardness, declining standards of health, even want of the most basic kind—too little food. Even today, the Soviet Union still cannot feed itself. After these four decades, then, there stands before the entire world one great and inescapable conclusion: Freedom leads to prosperity. Freedom replaces the ancient hatreds among the nations with comity and peace. Freedom is the victor.

Are Soviet Reforms Real?

And now the Soviets themselves may, in a limited way, be coming to understand the importance of freedom. We hear much from Moscow about a new policy of reform and openness. Some political prisoners have been released. Certain foreign news broadcasts are no longer being jammed. Some economic enterprises have been permitted to operate with greater freedom from state control.

Are these the beginnings of profound changes in the Soviet state? Or are they token gestures, intended to raise false hopes in the West, or to strengthen the Soviet system without changing it? We welcome change and openness; for we believe that freedom and security go together, that the advance of human liberty can only strengthen the cause of world peace. There is one sign the Soviets can make that would be unmistakable, that would advance dramatically the cause of freedom and peace.

General Secretary Gorbachev, if you seek peace, if you seek prosperity for the Soviet Union and Eastern Europe, if you seek liberalization: Come here to this gate! Mr. Gorbachev, open this gate! Mr. Gorbachev, tear down this wall!

VIEWPOINT 7

The Soviet Union Will Contribute to a New Kind of Revolution

Mikhail Gorbachev

The Cold War grew more tense in the early 1980s but then calmed down rapidly after 1985, with the fall of the Berlin Wall itself coming in November 1989. A major reason for the change in the nature of the Cold War, as well as for its ultimate end, was the reform effort begun by Mikhail Gorbachev in the Soviet Union. Only 54 years old, and therefore far younger than most other high-ranking Soviet officials, Gorbachev became the general secretary of the Soviet Communist Party in March 1985, and therefore the country's effective head of state. Gorbachev instituted reforms often referred to using the Russian words *glasnost* (openness) and *perestroika* (restructuring) in order to revive the Soviet economy and political culture, which had fallen into stagnation and disarray. By 1988 the larger reform movement had spread to some of the Soviet satellite nations in Eastern Europe.

SOURCE. Mikhail Gorbachev, "Address to the 43rd United Nations General Assembly," in http://isc.temple.edu, December 7, 1988.

The following selection consists of excerpts from a speech Gorbachev gave before the United Nations General Assembly in December 1988. In it, he added to his comments on general reforms the unexpected announcement that the Soviet Union, of its own accord, was going to greatly reduce its military presence in several of its friendly satellites, including East Germany. Therefore the East German government could no longer rely on Soviet military might to support the Berlin Wall and its restrictions. This announcement, as well as Gorbachev's readiness to discuss other forms of disarmament, helped pave the way for the collapse of East Germany and the fall of the Berlin Wall less than a year later. Gorbachev remained in power until the Soviet Union itself dissolved and rejected communism in 1991.

Our country is undergoing a truly revolutionary upsurge. The process of restructuring is gaining pace. We started by elaborating the theoretical concepts of restructuring; we had to assess the nature and scope of the problems, to interpret the lessons of the past, and to express this in the form of political conclusions and programs. This was done. The theoretical work, the re-interpretation of what had happened, the final elaboration, enrichment, and correction of political stances have not ended. They continue. However, it was fundamentally important to start from an overall concept, which is already now being confirmed by the experience of past years, which has turned out to be generally correct and to which there is no alternative.

In order to involve society in implementing the plans for restructuring it had to be made more truly democratic. Under the badge of democratization, restructuring has now encompassed politics, the economy, spiritual life, and ideology. We have unfolded a radical economic reform, we have accumulated experience, and from the new year we are transferring the entire national economy to new forms and work methods. Moreover, this means a profound reorganization of production relations and the

> The Soviet Union has made a decision on reducing its armed forces.

realization of the immense potential of socialist property.

In moving toward such bold revolutionary transformations, we understood that there would be errors, that there would be resistance, that the novelty would bring new problems. We foresaw the possibility of breaking in individual sections. However, the profound democratic reform of the entire system of power and government is the guarantee that the overall process of restructuring will move steadily forward and gather strength.

We completed the first stage of the process of political reform with the recent decisions by the U.S.S.R. Supreme Soviet on amendments to the Constitution and the adoption of the Law on Elections. Without stopping, we embarked upon the second stage of this. At which the most important task will be working on the interaction between the central government and the republics, settling relations between nationalities on the principles of Leninist internationalism bequeathed to us by the great revolution and, at the same time, reorganizing the power of the Soviets locally. We are faced with immense work. At the same time we must resolve major problems.

We are more than fully confident. We have both the theory, the policy and the vanguard force of restructuring a party which is also restructuring itself in accordance with the new tasks and the radical changes throughout society. And the most important thing: all peoples and all generations of citizens in our great country are in favor of restructuring. . . .

A Momentous Announcement

Today I can inform you of the following: The Soviet Union has made a decision on reducing its armed forces. In the next two years, their numerical strength will be reduced by 500,000 persons, and the volume of conventional arms will also be cut considerably. These reductions will be made on a unilateral basis, unconnected with negotiations on the mandate for the Vienna meeting. By agreement with our allies in the Warsaw Pact, we have made the decision to withdraw six tank divisions from the GDR [German Democratic Republic, or East Germany], Czechoslovakia, and Hungary, and to disband them by 1991. Assault landing formations and units, and a number of others, including assault river-crossing forces, with their armaments and combat equipment, will also be withdrawn from the groups of Soviet forces situated in those countries. The Soviet forces situated in those countries will be cut by 50,000 persons, and their arms by 5,000 tanks. All remaining Soviet divisions on the territory of our allies will be reorganized. They will be given a different structure from today's which will become unambiguously defensive, after the removal of a large number of their tanks. . . .

By this act, just as by all our actions aimed at the demilitarization of international relations, we would also like to draw the attention of the world community to another topical problem, the problem of changing over from an economy of armament to an economy of disarmament. Is the conversion of military production realistic? I have already had occasion to speak about this. We believe that it is, indeed, realistic. For its part, the Soviet Union is ready to do the following: Within the framework of the economic reform we are ready to draw up and submit our internal plan for conversion, to prepare in the course of 1989, as an experiment, the plans for the conversion of two or three defense enterprises, to publish our experience of job relocation of specialists from the military industry, and also of using its equipment, buildings, and works in civilian industry. It is desirable that all states, primarily the major military powers, submit their national plans on this issue to the United Nations.

It would be useful to form a group of scientists, entrusting it with a comprehensive analysis of problems of conversion as a whole and as applied to individual countries and regions, to be reported to the U.N. secretary-general, and later to examine this matter at a General Assembly session.

Reducing the Threat of War

Finally, being on U.S. soil, but also for other, understandable reasons, I cannot but turn to the subject of our relations with this great country. . . . Relations between the Soviet Union and the United States of America span five-and-a-half decades. The world has changed, and so have the nature, role, and place of these relations in world politics. For too long they were built under the banner of confrontation, and sometimes of hostility, either open or concealed. But in the last few years, throughout the world people were able to heave a sigh of relief, thanks to the changes for the better in the substance and atmosphere of the relations between Moscow and Washington.

No one intends to underestimate the serious nature of the disagreements, and the difficulties of the problems which have not been settled. However, we have already graduated from the primary school of instruction in mutual understanding and in searching for solutions in our and in the common interests. The U.S.S.R. and the United States created the biggest nuclear missile arsenals, but after objectively recognizing their responsibility, they were able to be the first to conclude an agreement on the reduction and physical destruction of a proportion of these weapons, which threatened both themselves and everyone else.

> The movement toward a nuclear-free and nonviolent world is capable of fundamentally transforming the political and spiritual face of the planet.

Both sides possess the biggest and the most refined military secrets. But it is they who have laid the basis for and are developing a system of mutual verification with regard to both the destruction and the limiting and banning of armaments production. It is they who are amassing experience for future bilateral and multilateral agreements. We value this. . . .

We are not inclined to oversimplify the situation in the world. Yes, the tendency toward disarmament has

The reforms of Soviet leader Mikhail Gorbachev (depicted on placard) made the fall of the Berlin Wall possible. **(Tom Stoddart/Hulton Archive/Getty Images.)**

received a strong impetus and this process is gaining its own momentum, but it has not become irreversible. Yes, the striving to give up confrontation in favor of dialogue and cooperation has made itself strongly felt, but it has by no means secured its position forever in the practice of international relations. Yes, the movement toward a nuclear-free and nonviolent world is capable of fundamentally transforming the political and spiritual face of the planet, but only the very first steps have been taken. Moreover, in certain influential circles, they have been greeted with mistrust, and they are meeting resistance.

The inheritance of inertia of the past are continuing to operate. Profound contradictions and the roots of many conflicts have not disappeared. The fundamental fact remains that the formation of the peaceful period will take place in conditions of the existence and rivalry of various socioeconomic and political systems. However, the meaning of our international efforts, and one of the key tenets of the new thinking, is precisely to impart to this rivalry the quality of sensible competition in conditions of respect for freedom of choice and a balance of interests. In this case it will even become useful and productive from the viewpoint of general world development; otherwise, if the main component remains the arms race, as it has been till now, rivalry will be fatal. Indeed, an ever greater number of people throughout the world, from the man in the street to leaders, are beginning to understand this.

Esteemed Mr. Chairman, esteemed delegates: I finish my first speech at the United Nations with the same feeling with which I began it: a feeling of responsibility to my own people and to the world community. We have met at the end of a year that has been so significant for the United Nations, and on the threshold of a year from which all of us expect so much. One would like to believe that our joint efforts to put an end to the era of wars, confrontation and regional conflicts, aggression against

Glasnost and Perestroika

From 1985 to 1991, the Soviet Union underwent major reforms that spread quickly to the Soviet satellite nations in Eastern Europe. These reforms were categorized using the Russian terms *glasnost* and *perestroika*.

Glasnost, means "openness." Soviet leader Mikhail Gorbachev, who had risen to power in 1985, was once quoted as saying, "I detest lies," and he wanted to provide for more freedom of speech and expression in what, until this period, was a mostly closed society. Glasnost was to result in the lifting of some censorship, greater freedom in political debate, and more transparency in the workings of government and bureaucracy.

Perestroika means "restructuring." By it, Gorbachev had in mind political and economic changes. He hoped to introduce certain democratic functions and institutions into what had been a single party state with a top-down style of governance. For instance, Gorbachev wanted elections to allow voters to choose from a slate of candidates rather than to simply rubber-stamp Communist Party ones. In the first such elections, in March of 1989, Soviet leaders were surprised to see voters reject doctrinaire Communists in favor of potential reformers.

In economics, perestroika allowed for free market reforms such as complete private ownership of certain businesses. Soviet entrepreneurs stepped up and opened their own restaurants or shops, but other, larger restrictions meant that the Soviet economy as a whole continued to stagnate. Indeed, as conditions worsened, increasing numbers of Soviet citizens used the greater openness to call for even more restructuring, with results that Gorbachev would not have foreseen.

nature, the terror of hunger and poverty, as well as political terrorism, will be comparable with our hopes. This is our common goal, and it is only by acting together that we may attain it. Thank you.

VIEWPOINT 8

The Possibility of German Reunification Should Inspire Caution

Arthur Miller

The following selection is from an article written by well-known twentieth-century American playwright Arthur Miller. In it he expresses concern over what might happen once East Germany is reunified with West Germany, an event that actually happened quickly following the fall of the Berlin Wall. Indeed, the two Germanys were united by October 1990 as a larger Federal Republic of Germany. The city of Berlin was reorganized as a single city once again as well, and it was restored as the capital of the Federal Republic in 1991, although it was not until 1999 that all governmental operations were in place there.

Miller's great concern, as indicated in the selection, was that Germany did not have a tradition of democratic government that had arisen from within the German population itself. Instead, democracy had been imposed on West Germany by the victors of World War II. Miller wondered whether democratic

---

SOURCE. Arthur Miller, "Uneasy About the Germans," *The New York Times*, May 6, 1990. Copyright © 1990 by The New York Times Company. Reprinted with permission.

institutions would hold or whether a united Germany would return to its authoritarian past.

Arthur Miller's best-known plays include *The Crucible, All My Sons,* and *Death of a Salesman.* He won the Pulitzer Prize for drama in 1949.

Do Germans accept responsibility for the crimes of the Nazi era? Is their repentance such that they can be trusted never to repeat the past? When people worry about the unification of Germany, these are the usual questions. But for me there is a deeper mystery, and it concerns the idea of nationhood itself in the German mind.

Three attempts to create a successful state have been smashed to bits in the mere 72 years since Germany's defeat in 1918. And although we are now in the presence of a great victory of a democratic system over a one-party dictatorship, it is not a democratic system of German invention. The nation about to be born is one that never before existed. And in apprehension over what this may mean, the Jews are by no means alone. The British are concerned and so are the French, not to speak of the Russians and numerous others whose lives were mined by German aggression.

I have more than the usual contact with Germans and German-speaking people. My wife, Austrian by birth, spent the war years in Germany, and her family is involved in German industry; I have German journalist friends, as well as colleagues in the German theater and the film and publishing industries. If I were to announce that I am not too worried about unification and have confidence in the democratic commitments of the younger generation, my friends would doubtless be happy to hear it—and proceed to worry privately on their own.

No one can hope to predict what course any country will take. I believe that for Germans, including those who

> 'To become democratic, is it enough to want a good job and a car?'

are eager for unification, the future of German democracy is as much of an enigma [mystery] as it is for the rest of us. They simply don't know. More precisely, they are almost sure it will turn out all right. But that's a big almost.

Several weeks ago in West Berlin, one of my wife's high school friends, a woman in her late 60's who never left Germany through the rise of Nazism, the war and reconstruction, had some conflicted, if not dark, things to say about the question. "In Germany it will always be the same," she said. "We go up very high but in the end we come down. We are winning and winning and winning, and then we lose. And when we are in trouble we turn to authority; orders and work make us happiest."

An Uncertain Future

She is using a cane these days, after a fall on the ice. She has a broad-beamed peasant air, thinning hennaed hair, ruddy cheeks. A survivor of a battered generation, she seems to refer to her own observations rather than to things she has read. "We must go slowly with unification," she said. "It is all darkness in front of us." And if the future is murky to West Germans, she wondered: "What is in the minds of the East Germans? We don't know. For us it was bad enough. We had 12 years of dictatorship, but after that we have had nearly 50 years of democracy. They have had nothing but dictatorship since 1933. To become democratic, is it enough to want a good job and a car and to hate the left?"

She has come to visit, despite her injury, because in her circle it is hard to find an open-minded conversation. "I fear it is all very artificial," she said. "It is the same old story, in one sense. We are not like the French, the British, the Americans. We never created our own democracy, or even our own regime, like the Russians; ours was handed to us by the Allies, and we are handing it to the D.D.R. [East German] people. But we had a memory of democracy before Hitler. Even their fathers have no such memory now. Who will influence whom—we over them or they over us?"

> German society had to be started . . . from a pile of bricks under which the shameful past was to be buried.

She talks about the Republicans, a far-right extremist party that won 90,000 votes in the last West Berlin election after only a few months of existence. "People say they are nonsensical, a tiny minority," she said. "I remember the other tiny nonsensical minority and how fast it took over. And mind you, we are prosperous now. What happens if we run into hard times and unemployment?"

That conversation could be repeated as many times as you like in Germany. But it is entirely possible that two-thirds of the Germans—those under 50, who can barely recollect Nazism—have only the remotest connection with the woman's sentiments and underlying worry. So hostile are they to any government intrusion in their lives that some of them made it nearly impossible to conduct a national census a few years ago because the questions being asked seemed to threaten them with regimentation from on high. Questions had to be altered, and some census takers were even accompanied by inspectors to make sure more personal questions than those prescribed were not asked. . . .

The German break with Hitlerism, the last German-made system, had to be total and condign [deserved]. And German society had to be started almost literally from a pile of bricks under which the shameful past was to be buried, put out of mind, deeply discredited.

If these observations are in fact operative, and I cannot imagine how they can be proved or disproved as such, then what Germans lack now is the consecration by blood of their democratic state. The torrent of German

Playwright Arthur Miller questioned whether a reunified Germany would be sufficiently democratic. (Craig Filipacchi/Liaison/Getty Images.)

blood that has flowed in this era in the Hitler-launched wars was, in fact, to prevent any such state from coming into existence.

For me, this is what keeps sucking the life out of German protestations of a democratic faith and casts suspicion on the country's reassurances that its economic power is no menace to the world. The fact is, West German civic practice has been as democratic as any other society's for more than 40 years and is less repressive and all-controlling than, for example, that of France, whose bureaucracy is positively strangulating by comparison.

I know Germans who are as certain as it is possible to be about anything that democracy will hold; I know other Germans who do not believe that at all. The world, it seems to me, has no choice but to support the positive side of the split and to extend its hand to a democratic Germany. By giving it the recognition it deserves, German democracy can only be strengthened, while meeting it with endless suspicion may finally wither its hopes. A recent *New York Times*/CBS News poll shows a large majority of Americans in favor of reunification, a vote of confidence with which I agree. At the same time, no German should take umbrage at the reminder that his nation in a previous incarnation showed that it had aggressive impulses that brought death to 40 million people. This memory should not vanish: it is part of democratic Germany's defense against the temptation to gather around some new extreme nationalism in the future.

The Need to Remember Germany's Past

It does not really do any good to remind Germans of those horrendous statistics if the purpose is simply to gratify an impulse to punish. But it is necessary never to forget what nationalistic blood lust can come to, so that it will never happen again.

Likewise, German resentment at such reminders has to be understood. No one can live in a perpetual state of repentance without resentment. In the scale and profundity of its degradation Nazism has no equal in modern time, but each country has had some level of experience with contrition, some taste of it, as a repayment for oppression of other people. What if every nation guilty of persecution were to own up? Are we really prepared to believe in their remorse? And while penitence in the persecutors may be a moral necessity for

> What do I care if a Nazi says he's sorry?

those who survived victimization, it will not bring back the dead. So is it not infinitely more important that the descendants of persecutors demonstrate something more than contrition, namely political responsibility?

What do I care if a Nazi says he's sorry? I want to know what the Constitution and educational system of Germany are doing to defend democracy under possibly difficult future circumstances. That is important to me and to my children. It is equally important that democracy live not only in institutions but in the German heart. But in all candor how are we ever to know that it does, except as crises are faced in a democratic spirit?

The world has a right—its World War II dead have earned it the right—to reproach and criticize and make demands of Germans if and when they seem to revert to bad habits. The Germans are going to have to face for a long time to come the legacy of their last attempt to dominate other nations.

But there is another Germany—the Germany of high aspirations. It does truly exist, and it must be welcomed wholeheartedly in the hope that one day its permanent dominion over the country will be unquestioned by any fair-minded person. In short, the time has come to look the worst in the eye and to hope for the best.

VIEWPOINT 9

The Reunification of Germany Is Nothing to Fear

Josef Joffe

Germany was first unified as a modern nation-state in 1871 under the "Iron Chancellor" Otto von Bismarck. Its aggressiveness was a major factor in starting World War I (1914–1918), the most devastating war the world had yet seen. Some Germans, unhappy with the way World War I ended, brought the Nazi regime and Adolf Hitler to Germany in 1933 and brought the globe into World War II (1939–1945), an even more destructive conflict. Following World War II, Germans in East Germany continued to live under a dictatorship while those in West Germany found themselves under a democratic regime imposed by the United States, Great Britain, and France (as well as many sympathetic Germans). Therefore, following the fall of the Berlin Wall in November 1989 and the reunification of Germany in October 1990, a relatively new nation was once again revived. Some feared that its size, industrial might, and energy might lead it to try to dominate Europe once again.

SOURCE. Josef Joffe, "Reunification II: This Time, No Hobnail Boots," *The New York Times*, September 30, 1990.

In the following selection, German scholar and journalist Josef Joffe tries to lay these fears to rest. He argues that democracy had taken firm hold in the "Bonn-Berlin" government that was to take over, and that democratic institutions were reinforced by Germany's place in such multinational institutions as NATO and the European Community (now the European Union). He also claims that, by the late 20th century, industry and commerce had replaced the force of arms as the main arena of national competition and was making war irrelevant, at least in Europe.

Josef Joffe is the editor and publisher of *Die Zeit*, a major German newsweekly magazine. He is also an adjunct professor of political science at Stanford University and an associate in international studies at Harvard University.

> Reunification will be a thoroughly peaceful affair.

In 1871, Germany was unified, and a few years later, the *Times of London* editorialized darkly: "We feel that an enormous power for good or evil has risen up somewhat suddenly in the midst of us, and we watch with interested attention for signs of its character and intention."

On Wednesday [October 3, 1990], the world will watch "Reunification II"—and as anxiously as 120 years ago. Will the sequel be a repeat performance, starring a restless giant who has become too big for his turf? Will Germany '90 move from strength to arrogance, again bringing grief to Europe and the rest of the world?

Comparisons Are Unwarranted

The Bismarck [architect of German unification in 1871]-to-Hitler analogy is tempting but misleading. Just compare the opening scenes. In 1871, Germany was unified by "blood and iron"—in a war of aggression launched against France. Today, Germans and French are no longer archenemies but the best of friends. On

German reunification allowed its citizens and government to pursue economic power much more than military power. (**AP Images.**)

Wednesday, the loudest sounds to be heard in Berlin will be the whistling of fireworks, not the rumble of artillery. Reunification will be a thoroughly peaceful affair.

Not only is the overture different this time; the stage, script and actors have also changed beyond recognition. Take the lead player. In the Bismarckian Reich [1871–1918], democracy was shouldered aside by a Prussian-dominated state that unleashed an economic revolution while chaining down liberty and dissent. The Kaiser's [Germany's leader] message to the rising middle classes was: Go ahead and enrich yourselves, but leave the driving to us.

> After World War II the stage changed.

In the Weimar Republic [of 1919–1933], born in defeat and disgrace

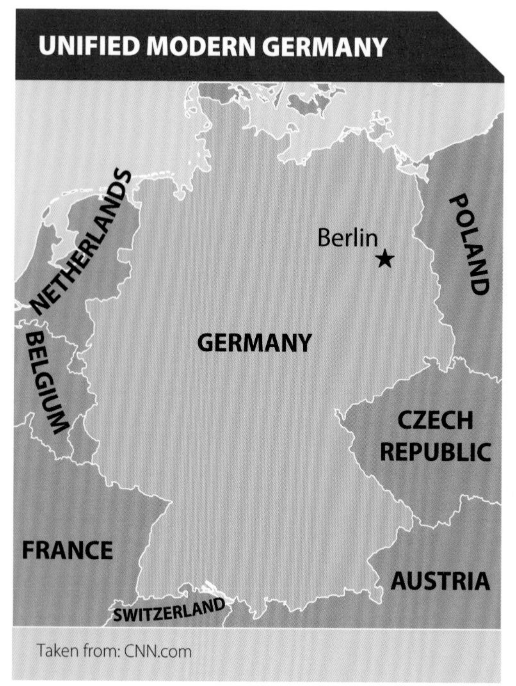

Taken from: CNN.com

after World War I, democracy never had a chance. Yes, there was a parliamentary regime, but it was ground down in a two-pronged attack by Communists and Nazis who flourished because millions were caught in the maw of the Great Depression. And in 1933, when Hitler came to power, democracy was simply torn to shreds.

After 1945 democracy could at last sink its roots into fertile soil, and in many ways the postwar political miracle in Germany even dwarfed its vaunted economic twin. This time, thanks to generous American help, democracy was not associated with economic misery and humiliation. Instead of reparations, there was Marshall Plan aid; instead of towering tariffs, there was free trade; instead of encirclement, there was NATO and the European Community, extending to the Germans a shelter and a role.

At last, then, German democracy was off to a good start, and today the Cassandras [prophets of doom] of 1945 have fallen silent. The parties of the extreme right and left have all but vanished, leaving in place a sluggishly centrist regime that is almost boring in its normalcy. The democratic system has weathered every political crisis: neo-Nazis and terrorists, insubordinate generals and rebellious students, large-scale unemployment and mass protests.

German Democracy Is Strong

In many respects, the political system looks like America writ small. Federalism works, and so does the separation of powers. Compared with the "republican monarchy" that is France, the Federal Republic is a political free-for-all. Nor is there an Official Secrets Act that so hampers the freedom of the press in Britain. State secrets in Bonn last about as long as in Washington—until tomorrow's edition.

The point is not that today's Germans are "good" whereas their grandfathers were thoroughbred authoritarians. The point is that after World War II the stage changed. Flawed as it was in the past, the drama of German history at last could unfold before a benign backdrop. Consider the ugly brew of paranoia and chauvinism that had poisoned the body politic before. The Bismarck Reich, a late arrival in the great power club, was bound to threaten all of its neighbors—and in turn to be threatened by them. The Weimar Republic was a pariah among nations and a target of endless distrust—a perfect breeding ground for the enemies of peace and democracy. It was "us against them" and "Deutschland Uber Alles" [Germany above all].

Reunified Germany, by contrast, will be embedded in a larger community, surrounded by friends and not by resentful neighbors. The Federal Republic grew up in security, provided courtesy of the United States, and this cut down the business opportunities of the Pied Pipers. Try as they may, right-wing parties, hawking their message of hate, have never established a foothold in the Federal Parliament.

But, so the skeptics will demur, that wonderful edifice is collapsing before our own eyes. With the Soviet surrender in the Cold War, the Atlantic alliance is fading and the Americans are going home. Won't Germany, finally unshackled from its postwar fetters, again be tempted by sheer strength and the heady lure of aggrandizement?

True, waning dependence equals less deference. Absent the Soviet threat, Bonn-Berlin might be less hesitant to convert economic muscle into political clout. But to argue that Reunification II will turn into a remake

> "The battle lines are drawn in the balance-of-payments ledgers, and the accounts are settled with dollars and Deutsche marks, not blood and iron."

of the 1871 original is to ignore how much the script itself has changed.

New Forms of National Rivalry

The rivalry of nations in the democratic-industrial world has moved from the battlefield into the economic arena, and it promises to stay there as long as the marvelous economic community Europeans have built persists. Nobody expects the Germans to invade Alsace again; now they pay for the pleasure of owning the choice plots there, just as the Japanese are buying, not bombing, Pearl Harbor.

Power in Europe (as opposed to Saddam Hussein's neighborhood) is measured not by conquest but by capital surpluses. Not booty and glory define the stakes, but questions such as: "Who determines currency parities?" It so happens that the Bundesbank [the German National bank] calls the shots, which understandably grates hard on the French. But worlds separate this contest from the game played out with German jackboots in Paris 50 years ago. The battle lines are drawn in the balance-of-payments ledgers, and the accounts are settled with dollars and Deutsche marks, not blood and iron. The rivalry is about joint welfare, not this or that province; both sides lose or win together. (American victims of Sony resent cheap VCRs made in Japan, but who would go to war over the privilege of buying worse-quality goods at higher prices?) Still, might not Bonn-Berlin hanker after nuclear weapons and push for revision of its eastern borders? What for? The new, more civilized and civilianized game of nations offers the largest payoffs to nations such as Germany and Japan. The game has devalued the military chips, delivering power and prestige to those who can back up their bets with investments and loans. Why, then, should they forego their advantage by changing the rules? In the attempt, they would certainly revive the hostile coalitions that proved their undoing in 1945. Also, well-settled democracies are more sensible about such risks than were the Hohenzollerns [Kaisers] and Hitlerites.

On Wednesday, Bonn Inc. [West Germany] will take over bankrupt Prusso-Marx, a.k.a. East Germany. But the remake of 1871 will not be shot with a cast of latter-day Erich von Stroheims. The soundtrack will not be "Deutschland Uber Alles," but Beethoven's "Ode to Joy," Europe's unofficial anthem. Walking alone in the distant past, Germans easily fell for the mesmerizing music of the Pied Pipers. But in the meantime Europe has changed, and so has Germany. Hamburg and Rome, Munich and Marseilles have been listening to the same tune for a long time; adding Dresden and Leipzig [East German cities] should not ruin that score.

CHAPTER 3

Watching the Wall Come Down

VIEWPOINT 1

A Moment of Change at Checkpoint Charlie

Christopher Hilton

The Berlin Wall ceased to be a meaningful barrier on the evening of November 9, 1989. In the following selection, historian Christopher Hilton traces the events of that evening using the experiences and memories of a number of different people at the center of them. They include West Berliners at a café near the wall, East German border guards, and American soldiers assigned to Checkpoint Charlie, Hilton's setting. Checkpoint Charlie was one of the main gateways in the Berlin Wall, and the only one open to non-Germans or to Western military personnel. When the wall first went up in 1961, American and Soviet tanks stood face to face at the intersection later termed Checkpoint Charlie. By November 9, 1989, as Hilton notes, relations between the two superpowers were fairly routine but few on the scene were certain whether the East German government was truly lifting its border restrictions as West German radio and TV stations were suggesting. While those at the café celebrated, and took their celebration outside to the gathering

Photo on previous page: The flood of people through the fallen Berlin Wall on the night of November 9, 1989, left East German authorities powerless. **(AP Images.)**

SOURCE. Christopher Hilton, *The Wall: The People's Story*. Stroud, Gloucestershire, United Kingdom: Sutton Publishing, 2001.

crowds, the armed personnel from both sides found events overtaking them.

Christopher Hilton's many books include *Hitler's Olympics: The 1936 Berlin Olympic Games* and *Mayflower: The Voyage that Changed the World.*

Checkpoint Charlie, Between 7:30 and 8:00 P.M.

Of Astrid Benner's seven customers five were women who worked on a newspaper round the corner. They used the Café Adler as a haunt because it was conveniently close to mull over the doings of the day. They were talking about the woman's page. A photographer came in and said that 'in the next hour something will happen here'.

Astrid Benner wondered what he was talking about.

'Don't you know? They will open the border.'

The women didn't know either because the taped music had insulated them. One said 'Can you believe it? Let's listen to the radio.' Benner flipped the tape out, turned on the big box radio with its strong speakers and everyone heard it together, a recording of the laden voice of Schabowski seemingly coming at them from wherever Benner twisted the dial. All channels were carrying it and trying to wring a meaning from those final words about the lifting of travel restrictions.

The women, according to Benner, 'got excited and said, "We'd better get back to the office," and they started to run. I thought to myself, "What will I do now? I am by myself here." I called my boss, the owner of the café, at his home. "Hell," I said, "you have to get here because I am totally alone and thousands of people may be coming at any moment. This is the first place they'll reach. . . ."'

The owner, Albrecht Raw, made it inside 15 minutes with his wife, Nellie.

Like New Year's Eve

Outside, Benner saw 'a few people beginning to arrive from our side, the Western side. They stood round and some came into the café for a drink. A feeling grew like it was New Year's Eve, a sort of mounting excitement but nothing happened. We were listening to the radio, commentators were talking and talking but nothing happened. We felt it had to, and now, but it didn't.'

Across the line the checkpoint ticked evenly. The white light fell on its carpet, the binoculars tracked from the watchtowers. There was minimal movement under the Customs awning. The checkpoint presented itself as it had always done, set in its terrible permanence.

'When my boss and his wife arrived we wanted to drink champagne,' Astrid Benner says. 'Then I had an idea. *It's not just we who ought to be celebrating. The Border Guards should be celebrating, too. Let's give them some champagne.* My boss thought it was a good idea. I got a tray out and set about twenty glasses on it, he opened two bottles.'

Benner and Raw came down the three shallow steps of the café and turned towards the white line. An hour before, this would have been unthinkable and extremely dangerous: the Guards in the tower lurked like menacing presences behind the windows, trained to shoot. Benner and Raw crossed the white line, walking at a stately pace towards the watchtower. Benner didn't 'think of the possibility the Guards would shoot us because we were making such a friendly, open action and everybody could see it was not dangerous'. Something fundamental, she felt, had altered. As they walked, two Guards emerged from the watchtower and advanced urgently towards them. 'They wore grey uniforms. One stood in the background and the other came directly to us—always two Guards, one covering the other.'

The first intercepted Benner and Raw midway between the line and the tower. Astrid offered him champagne.

'Go back,' he said.

'But we have to celebrate this exciting day, don't you want to celebrate with us?'

'No, no, we don't want that, please go back again.'

'If you don't want to drink now take this bottle. You can drink it later.'

The Guard, Benner would remember, was 'severe just like the Border Guards were but I could sense he didn't know what to do. I assumed he had heard the news from the Press Conference but of course he might not. When it was obvious he wasn't going to accept any champagne we re-crossed the line and drank with the people standing there. By now, slowly, more and more people had gathered. Then we returned to the café and began to prepare for a big party. We went into the cellar to get glasses and telephoned anybody who might be able to lend a hand but either they didn't have time or they weren't at home. My boss's wife had never worked in this line of business but she said, "OK, I'll help." The Guards were back in their tower watching us through their binoculars.'

> They were selling champagne by the bottle in the Café Adler now.

After this innocent little flurry the checkpoint re-set itself in concrete.

Watching and Waiting

[Commander of East German border guards Günter] Moll's telephone rang. Simon [a subordinate] informed him that 'a waitress and a man from the Café Adler had come across the line and wanted the Border Guards to drink with them. The Guards had told them they were on duty and not allowed to drink, the waitress and the man had returned to the café. I told Major Simon it didn't seem a serious situation but to keep his eyes open and watch everything. If it did become serious he should call again.'

Far to the other side of the city [U.S. Army Major Bernie] Godek picked up [U.S. political military adviser Colonel John] Greathouse who told him about the press conference. It was a lengthy drive. They reached the checkpoint and 'there were just a few people in the area, as a matter of fact. It really didn't look much different to the way it looked on any evening. A few tourists always milled around. Some media personnel were there, some people were just lingering. We walked to the hut and spoke to [U.S. soldier] Sgt. Brown. The *imbiss* [the snack bar beside the Allied hut] was open and one or two people stood eating. Nothing unusual.'

Godek had those unseen eyes, the camera up on the side of the building above the café relaying every movement on the Eastern side to a screen in the hut as well as the Mitchell Suite [a U.S. observation post above the Adler Café]. 'Colonel Greathouse asked me to take him up there because he wanted to use the telephone. I unlocked the door and let him in so he could make some calls. I went back down to the checkpoint to monitor and sense what was going on. More and more people started showing up, more media started showing up.'

They were selling champagne by the bottle in the Café Adler now. . . .

Checkpoint Charlie, 8:00 to 8:30 P.M.

There was an inherent sense of theatre about this place and always had been. Since August 1961, it resembled a stage in the structure of its background, its foreground and its personnel who, in a sense, were actors moving in their allocated parts across it, never deviating from the script. This night the last act was being played out, obeying the formalised structure in which it was set.

By 8:00 only a few were congregating on the Eastern side of the checkpoint, but [more were] along the street at the rear of it because fear kept them from approaching. By 8:30, several hundred people had gathered on the Western side.

Elsewhere, as this was happening, the night began to touch people at random, and in differing ways.

Ernest Steinke was chief editor of RIAS [Radio In the American Sector] 1, the broadcasting station founded in 1946, but since 1968 a German and American broadcasting station. 'I worked in the Eastern section of this station and I saw the press conference on TV. I went to the studio afterwards to tell the people there what had happened. Somebody had asked [East Berlin Communist leader Günter] Schabowski when people could go over to the Western side and he said, "We have a new law, it's OK." Someone asked, "What time?" and he said, "I don't know but I think the law is ready and they can go now." He also said they had to have a passport and a visa. I went up two flights of stairs to the studio and people asked me what had happened. I said the people could come over and someone said, "There will be thousands coming, a hundred thousand." I pointed out that they had to have a visa, had to go to the police for a stamp and "the police will open tomorrow morning at eight o'clock, maybe, and there will be a lot of people going there. I guess about ten o'clock they'll start coming." Then I went home and went to bed to go back to RIAS early next morning. . . .'

RIAS radio reporter Peter Schultz felt 'the impression it made on me was even stronger than the night it had gone up—throughout the years, we had seen people dying at the wall, we'd seen people jumping out of the windows at Bernauer Strasse; I'd covered Peter Fechter [an 18-year-old killed for trying to cross the Berlin Wall in 1962]. After twenty-eight years of these experiences, there was nobody in Berlin who believed that the wall could come down again after a sud-

> 'We saw Guards coming out and although we really didn't know what to expect we figured it might turn into a nasty situation.'

den and comparatively short period: no journalist, no politician, *nobody*. When it happened it was—again—like a shock, but this time a positive shock. When I saw the press conference on TV I had an idea something would happen but I thought it would be the next morning. A football match was being televised [on Western television] and there was a flash that the wall was open and thousands of people were marching in the direction of the checkpoints. So I went to the radio station. . . .'

Checkpoint Charlie, 8:30 to 9:00 P.M.

In the Mitchell Suite, Yount [the Colonel's driver] and Greathouse watched. Yount phoned Godek in the hut and reported that he had noticed 'some vehicles coming into an open cement area at the back of the checkpoint and it looked as if they might be carrying East German soldiers. The vehicle movement brought about a lot of concern because the last time we had seen that they'd built the extension to the front of the checkpoint. We saw Guards coming out and although we really didn't know what to expect we figured it might turn into a nasty situation.'

They were Guards not soldiers. Moll had sensed days before that, with the government truly floundering and demonstrations on the streets, he might need reinforcements and had requested sixty of them. They were armed. . . .

Checkpoint Charlie, 9:30 P.M.

Moll's deputy rang again and said about a hundred people, some foreigners, had gathered on the other side of the line and were imploring the Guards to please let the people from the East come through. 'I told him to make sure that everything remained quiet, that law and order was maintained. I told him it was his duty to ensure that normal traffic—the cars and buses—should continue to cross as usual. I added, "I will be there as soon as pos-

The mood at the border crossings was festive the day the Berlin Wall fell on November 9, 1989. **(AP Images.)**

sible. . . .'" Within a few minutes Moll got into his Skoda [a Czech car] and set off on the journey back. . . .

Checkpoint Charlie, 10:30 P.M.

Greathouse asked Godek if 'we would be willing to venture through the crowds with our vehicle to exercise our right of free access because by then it was essentially a mass of people out in front of the hut. Sgt. Yount and someone else attempted to go through but they had to stop. The crowd was solid. Not far behind Yount was a Soviet vehicle with four uniformed soldiers in it—they had been over in the West for whatever reason—and they were trapped maybe four, maybe five vehicles behind ours. Finally this Soviet vehicle caught the attention of some of the crowd who started rocking it, which to us seemed rather unusual because they didn't show that reaction to Sergeant Yount in ours.'

Inside the Café Adler, Astrid Benner heard 'screaming begin, just screaming. I couldn't tell what they were screaming.' It was the crowd, and the screaming actually a chant deep from the pits of many stomachs.

'By now the Guards didn't look aggressive and they had not a clue what was going on.'

A Crowd Gathers

Moll moved to the front of the checkpoint and tried to calm the 2,000, 3,000. A flashbulb burst nearby and the moment was captured for the morning newspaper. 'Already I had a feeling that this could not go on. Something had to happen. I knew my men would not be able to hold them back, it was not possible, so they withdrew behind the wall.'

This 'totally surprised' Godek. Border Guards did not withdraw in the face of a crowd. Quite the opposite, they fronted it out.

By 10:45, ZDF and ARD [West German television] were broadcasting that the checkpoints at Bornholmer Strasse, Sonnenallee and Invalidenstrasse would open. What was happening at Bornholmer Strasse and Checkpoint Charlie was being duplicated at each of the other checkpoints; and at each, as the structures of obedience broke down, Border Guards and passport controls were facing extraordinary decisions unaided. Their predicament was not helped by the singular fact that they had spent their careers *not* really making any decisions at all, never mind anything like this.

A photographer at Checkpoint Charlie noted that 'by now the Guards didn't look aggressive and they had not a clue what was going on. You could see that on their faces. They didn't pull back behind the wall in formation. They looked very undecided among themselves. First one or two pulled back, then a few more, then a few more. . . .'

They vacated the wedge of road between the white line and the wall itself. In a few moments around ten

Westerners moved across the white line through the barricade and up to the wall. Within seconds thirty or forty more followed and then, in a vast slow-rippling wave, more followed.

Confused Guards and Soldiers

Moll walked briskly to the watchtower and telephoned headquarters a third time. No new regulations. At this instant, with so many people so near and more and more arriving, Commander Günter Moll was the loneliest of men. He did not know that what was happening here was happening at the six other checkpoints simultaneously, that a great current flowed through the city. The checkpoints had no direct communication with each other for security reasons, so that no one could coordinate a mass exodus or indeed coordinate anything at all. He gave the order to close the small pedestrian gate. Sealing the vehicle gate would have represented violation of the Four Power Agreement and risked escalation of the situation.

Sergeant Yount struggled through the crowd and moved past the line of Border Guards, crossed the checkpoint, followed by the Soviet vehicle, returned after what seemed a long time and reported that yes, a crowd had gathered in the East, they were very quiet but he sensed anticipation.

Obedience had been studiously bred into them, waiting was what they did, mute and uncomplaining. It was never wise to complain. None of them put a foot inside the checkpoint, none made an intrusion.

In the hut Greathouse took a decision and informed Godek of it. 'He decided that we did not need to be accessed. We accepted a point in time where our access would be completely blocked—by ordinary people. I was with the Colonel when he made the decision and it was based on two factors: the emotions of the people on our side and the reactions of the Border Guards. Their conduct changed shortly after 11:00. The crowd started crossing the line in a mass from our side, something completely unheard of before. People meandered over, people tried to climb up onto the wall. The first couple were initially asked by the Guards to "please come off it" but there was no physical contact at all, they weren't dragged off. Eventually enough people were up on the wall that the Guards just let them sit there.'

A Border Ceases to Exist

The current had reached here, unspoken, unregulated, spontaneous—but here. These people on the wall sat with their legs draped down, almost lolled, casual as you like.

Godek continues: 'Just in front of one of the watchtowers, the one to the left as we looked at it, there was a little grassy area and the crowd started milling on that and the Guards let them sit there. Then people sat on the wall next to the watchtower actually looking in at the Guards, something else completely unheard of. The mood was jovial, almost carnival. When Sgt. Yount came back from his last sweep Colonel Greathouse said, "We don't need to press our rights, we need to just let this happen. This is a moment for the German people."'

The current caught the Guards and embraced them: a lover's embrace.

'Some of the Guards took their hats off and threw them into the crowd. I couldn't believe it. People were talking with them, they were talking with the people which they had always been prohibited from doing. We saw smiles on their faces.' Major Godek was a calm and conscientious man. He read the implications of these little gestures perfectly. He knew.

One of the Westerners grabbed the cap of a Guards officer, put it on and stood laughing. The officer said, 'Please may I have it back, I need it or I'll be in trouble.' The cap was returned. At this instant, the wedge of road was a solid sea of Westerners, the full 2,000, and

> Moll risked his career and quite possibly his life when he said, 'I am opening the border.'

they pressed against the low wall, although gently, no push and shove, almost no jostling. Behind it the Guards—nearly all capless—stood milling. Hands reached across to try and shake theirs. This low wall was of wood and three Guards pressed their hands against it to stop the pressure of the 2,000 from tipping it over. Someone wearing trainers and an anorak clambered onto it from the West and stood precariously beside the pedestrian gate, turned back to the West and, arms outstretched, gestured as if to say 'Well, what are you waiting for?' That was greeted by reverberating laughter among the 2,000.

Two stout supports flanked the pedestrian gate and Moll—he had his cap, he still looked as if his uniform had been moulded to him—clambered onto one of them, surveyed the sea which had flowed to just in front of him. His arms were slack at his sides. As he surveyed, he knew. Nearby a photographer asked a Guard to haul him up onto the wall so he could take pictures from both sides and was deeply astonished that the Guard did. . . .

Checkpoint Charlie, Toward Midnight

The impression that 'something had to happen' was growing stronger and stronger on Moll. 'The crowd were calling to each other, "Let us go! Let us go!"' He was under an arch of sound, a chant rising from the West—'Come! Come! Come!'—and echoing back from the East—'We're coming! We're coming! We're coming!' He made a fourth and final call.

In the hut Godek watched. Greathouse departed to see developments elsewhere in the city but, before he did, he said the word was that the checkpoint would open, sometime. 'He also informed us that we had been receiving reports of crowds forming at some of the other crossing points. My British counterpart, Major Ross Mackay, stopped by. He'd been to the Brandenburg Gate—which was in the British Sector—and some of his crossing points and he reported the same kind of atmosphere.

An American Officer Remembers

'If anything impressed me it was the completely different attitude of the Guards, their change in behaviour. It was the fact that they tossed their hats into the crowd, these same Guards I had seen during previous demonstrations with their stone faces. They were being offered champagne, they were being offered beer. They didn't accept anything but they were laughing. One Guard had his hat removed by someone sitting on the wall and didn't make any attempt to get it back.'

The current exposed the Border Guards for what they were: people.

In the Café Adler Astrid Benner heard 'the noise grow and grow. We could see the Guards in the watchtower still using their binoculars but you knew they didn't know what to do except keep doing that.' . . .

Moll made his call. No new regulations. 'I felt pressure from the people calling to each other but I also felt pressure from history.'

Moll walked briskly from the watchtower to the Customs and spoke to the most senior officer. Moll knew nothing of this officer, not even his name. Moll risked his career and quite possibly his life when he said, 'I am opening the border.' He could not do it without the Stasi [East Germany's secret police]. What might happen if he said the people could come through and the Stasi, occupying the strategic middle ground under the awning, said they could not? It was the Stasi, not Moll, who would have to consent, would have to open the rear gate of the checkpoint to allow the people to shuffle forward in their obedience; the Stasi who would have to stamp all the passports with exit visas; and the Stasi were still undiluted. What if they struck at Moll? He faced essentially the same dilemma as [East German Passport official Harald] Jäger, although Jäger was Stasi himself. Someone had to make the decision.

'Open It.'

Moll waited this last, final moment for the passport controller to reply. The passport controller said, 'Yes.'

That was all.

Godek sensed the current and knew it was now. Why, he asked himself, interfere with it? He heard the shouting in the East but 'from the distance away that we were, we couldn't tell what they were shouting.'

Moll walked from the awning to where his reinforcements stood; walked to the pedestrian gate and gave the order very quietly, without any sense of theatre.

'Open it.'

The Guard manning the gate obeyed. It was a tactical move which would allow people from the West an entry point. At the same time Moll's men lined up again but this time in a different formation: a diagonal.

Toft's radio crackled and he wrote on his piece of paper: '2359 hours. Small build up of East Germans at Checkpoint. Approx. twenty East German Border Guards present.'

In a certain sense this was one of the last messages transmitted when the cold war was still cold.

Godek, watching his TV monitor intently, saw the crowd in the East move from the road towards and through the narrow gate at the back of the checkpoint, saw them entering the Customs area. This crowd, orderly and in line, were now where Godek's TV could no longer follow them. Customs was under the awning and enclosed.

It was, truly, a minute before midnight on Thursday 9 November 1989 or a minute or two into Friday 10 November. There is no precision about the timing because there is no exact moment, no instant which would have to be developed, carefully printed, fixed. The current was a progression of moments flowing one to another.

At midnight the Invalidenstrasse checkpoint opened. East Berlin itself was open for the first time since midnight, 13 August 1961.

VIEWPOINT 2

The Fall of the Wall Had Both Political and Personal Meaning

Richard von Weizsaecker

The following selection is from a memoir written by Richard von Weizsaecker, president of the Federal Republic of Germany from 1984 to 1994, a period that included the fall of the Berlin Wall and the reunification of West and East Germany. In the German system, the president is considered the head of state while the chancellor, a different office, is the head of the government itself. Germany's chancellor at the time was Helmut Kohl, like Weizsaecker, a politician held in high esteem both in Germany and around the world.

In this selection, the former president recounts how the removal of border restrictions in parts of Eastern Europe in 1988 and 1989 had resulted in a new flood of East German migrants to the West, and how attempted crackdowns on these migrants had inspired the protests that helped to lead to the fall of the wall. He also remembers what the wall's end meant

---

SOURCE. Richard von Weizsaecker, *From Weimar to the Wall: My Life in German Politics*. New York: Broadway Books, 1999.

to him both personally and as a politician connected to events across Europe and the world. At the heart of Weizsaecker's account is his strong sense of the unity of the German people on both sides of the disappearing border.

Exciting events now occurred in East Germany almost daily. The situation was in the hands of the people, while the political leaders had a hard time responding promptly, keeping their wits about them, and holding on to their nerve. [East German leader Erich] Honecker had just affirmed that the Wall would still be standing in fifty or a hundred years, as long as the reasons for its construction remained valid. But in June 1988 the Hungarian foreign minister, Gyula Horn, and his Austrian counterpart, Alois Mock, symbolically cut the barbed-wire fence marking the frontier near Sopron. When the wave of "vacationers" from East Germany crested soon after, West German embassies in Budapest, Prague, and Warsaw were filled with them. The problems of finding enough provisions and maintaining hygiene for these crowds grew beyond anything imaginable in these havens. A flurry of contacts flowed between Bonn and the governments involved. These involved dramatic negotiations, with the active participation of the East German attorney Wolfgang Vogel in Prague and East Berlin. They resulted in Genscher's and Seiters's [both West German officials] traveling to Prague in late September to bring their countrymen, crowded into the embassy grounds, the liberating news that their path to the Federal Republic had been cleared. This moment marked the first of the radical changes.

Starting in early September, each Monday saw demonstrations outside the Nikolai Church in Leipzig. The demonstrators' banners were emblazoned "Freedom to Travel, Not Mass Flight." On September 9 the first countrywide opposition movement, called New Forum, was founded at the home of Robert Havemann's widow, Bärbel Bohley and Jens Reich were among the members [the three were East German dissidents].

To commemorate the fortieth anniversary of the founding of the German Democratic Republic [GDR] on October 7, [Soviet leader Mikhail] Gorbachev visited East Berlin. Once more his conflict with Honecker over the need for reform led to heated disagreement. Gorbachev did not understand why East Berlin resisted following the example of other socialist countries. He may have underestimated how much more difficult this step was for the SED [East Germany's ruling party] leadership than it was for Hungary or Poland, because it demanded a perspective that saw Germany as one nation, and this outlook the SED could not want.

At his Berlin press conference Gorbachev, using his vivid vocabulary, casually dropped a phrase that became part of our stock of frequent citations: "If you come too late, life will punish you." Later he told me that his intention was not to provide us with a familiar quotation. What mattered, he said, was the realization that history itself makes all the decisions, and trying to anticipate it was as futile as expecting to profit by missing the moment. He insisted that he had held the same opinion during our meeting in the Kremlin in 1987, when he had deflected my question on German unity by talking about the workings of history. It is crucial for statesmen to understand in good time where history is headed. This was what he meant by his statement in East Berlin; he had mostly been talking to himself.

Peaceful Protests

Immediately after Gorbachev's visit the largest and most dramatic demonstrations were held in numerous East German cities, once again primarily in Leipzig; "We Are the People," "No Force," "This Is Where We Stay," the banners read. The strain was unimaginable. All of

Germany sat glued to the television screen. All Germans near and far held their breath; but no shots were fired by either side. The Soviets had managed to avoid a bloodbath during this momentous provocation. Unlike the Chinese government, which had shortly before used deadly force against the students in Tiananmen Square in Beijing, the Soviets ordered all troops to remain in their barracks. These marked the decisive hours of Germany's peaceful revolution. It was a success.

> On November 4 [1988] the largest demonstration, seven hundred thousand people, was staged on Berlin's Alexanderplatz with police approval.

On October 17 Honecker was ousted and Egon Krenz became his successor. The demands on the banners immediately changed to "Unlimited Freedom." On November 4 the largest demonstration, seven hundred thousand people, was staged on Berlin's Alexanderplatz with police approval. A colorful mix of writers, an actress, a clergyman, and two leading SED members spoke. "Flowers, Not Borders," "Legal Security Makes State Security Unnecessary," and "We Are the People—You Are the Ones Who Should Leave" were seen on a large banners. German unity was not yet a topic of slogans.

No one knew what would happen next. On November 8 [West German leader Helmut] Kohl made an official visit to Poland of several days' duration while I fulfilled obligations in southern Germany. On the evening of November 9, shortly before 7 P.M., Günter Schabowski, a member of the Berlin SED politburo, announced that beginning immediately short-term "travel abroad" would be granted. The barriers dividing Berlin were raised after 11 P.M., and that same night huge crowds thronged past the old, hated obstacles. There was no end to the joyous outbursts. "Last night the German people were the happiest people in the world," Governing Mayor Walter Momper stated on November 10 outside the Schöneberg city hall. Never before and never since in my lifetime have I seen an event on German soil literally gladden the entire world, which shared our joy.

Watching Barriers Come Down

Three moments remain most vivid in my memory from the following days, which I spent in Berlin. The first thing I did was cross the Glienick Bridge, which crosses the Havel and is the only pedestrian connection between West Berlin and Potsdam. This bridge had constricted us into West Berlin for decades, sealing us off even more hermetically than the midtown sector crossings. Only the Four Powers could use the bridge. This was where the now famous exchanges of [US, Soviet, British, and French] spies took place between the two sides, among them Francis Gary Powers, the U-2 pilot shot down over the Soviet Union [in 1961]. But the courageous Russian dissident Nathan Sharanski had also walked this path to freedom. Many times I participated in a custom unique to West Berliners. On weekends we would drive along the Potsdamer Chaussee toward the bridge, only to bump our heads, as it were, against the barricade at the center of the bridge, where the barriers and guards forbade us access to Potsdam—a place I came to know well as a boy and where my garrison was based—and the Mark Brandenburg. We felt like animals caged behind bars. And now, strolling across the bridge and back again with big smiles on our faces, we gave in to our feelings. It was as if we all knew each other.

At the city's center I went to the Potsdamer Platz, still a big, empty square controlled by guards on both sides. All alone I crossed from the west, a distance of 200 meters to the other side, where the barracks of the Volkspolizei (People's Police) were located. What would happen? A guard unit watched my approach through a telescope. Then the head of the unit, a lieutenant,

> "No one wanted to go home. Everyone was ready to share."

peeled off from his men, marched toward me, saluted smartly, and calmly said, "Reporting, Federal President: No uncommon occurrences." We saluted each other as if our encounter were the most ordinary thing in the world, though we were living through an event that could not have been more unusual.

The third day after the Wall was breached I took part in the Sunday service in the Gedächtniskirche [the "memorial church," West Berlin], which was overflowing with people from East and West. My bishop, Martin Kruse, with whom I had a very close relationship, asked me to address the congregation at the end of the service. My speech, which turned out to be an awkward mixture of lay devotion and a welcome to Berliners from both parts of the city, was based on St. Paul's words to the Galatians, which I had come to cherish during the Protestant Conferences. The verses read, "Stand fast therefore in the liberty wherewith Christ hath made us free, and be not entangled again with the yoke of bondage. . . . For, brethren, ye have been called unto liberty; only use not liberty for an occasion to the flesh, but by love serve one another." In speaking, I was thinking primarily of residents in the West. Their duty was to be ready with open doors and hearts instead of blundering into other territory and insisting that their opinions and values were the only valid ones. What East Germany needed now was not high-flown words but aid. "None of us knew ahead of time—none of us knows what will happen next. . . . The people show the way to politics. When politics is a concern of the people, it deals with the liberty humankind longs for and with the responsibility without which liberty leads to license. Responsibility means solidarity one with the other, the solidarity in which liberty is fulfilled—love, as we Christians say. Let us stand fast in this kind of liberty." These words were the first signal of things to come: Those who would unite must learn to share.

A huge crowd gathered outside the church after the service. We could not sort ourselves out by Eastern or Western origin and had no wish to do so. We crushed and cherished each other. No one wanted to go home. Everyone was ready to share.

Next Step: Verification

This was how the first radical change in Germany was completed. The second was still not clearly identifiable. While other nations tapped around in the dark, Kohl discreetly took the initiative on November 28 in the Bundestag by launching his ten-point program, which [National Security Adviser] Horst Teltschik had detailed for me the previous day. Kohl spoke of the stages we must follow to arrive at unity and announced his readiness to take up a proposal by East Germany's prime minister, Hans Modrow, for a "treaty community." Further, he suggested that "confederative structures between the two German states" be developed with the ultimate goal of federation, and he defined the political objective as Germany's national unity. On the road to this goal, he suggested, no one could now give correct and conclusive answers to the many difficult questions that would arise.

Reaction to this program among the neighboring capitals and Four Powers was at first mixed. Paris expressed irritation because three days earlier, during a private dinner with [French President François] Mitterrand, Kohl had given no indication of his plan. Washington too would have preferred being informed ahead of time instead of receiving formal notification immediately after the speech. The following day [U.S.] Secretary of State [James] Baker had a clever explanation for the way the event unfolded: To unite Germany, the road of self-determination was essential; but the legal position and responsibility of the Allies must be properly observed. Unification must come about gradually and peacefully, and the permanent German obligation to NATO and the European Community must be preserved; therefore unification could not be bought with neutrality. After all, the inviolability of borders had to be observed, a concern Kohl had not addressed. Baker thus focused on the missing piece in Kohl's ten points, relating to Poland's western border, an omission noted everywhere, especially abroad. By verbalizing the problem, the United States contributed to easing tensions and plainly indicated the direction negotiations must take in the immediate future.

The East German leadership was in turmoil. With Krenz still general secretary of the SED, the Volkskammer [People's Chamber or Parliament] canceled the party's leadership set forth in the constitution and openly debated numerous past abuses of authority and instances of corruption. The situation was quite unprecedented. On the one hand the GDR's constitution kept it from even approaching democracy. On the other, new impulses were sparked by the people far more than in an established democracy as practiced in the West. Actually, it was as if the authority to set directions for policy lay in the hands of the people. Mainly it was the people who manifested the radical change and decisive force in the GDR at the inception of unification.

Immediately before Kohl announced his ten-point program, the first public demands for national unification were heard in East Germany. Until that time most popular phrases had called for an independent GDR with such slogans as "Don't sell out the GDR" and "We won't be Federordered around [a reference to West Germany's Federal Republic]." Now increasing public demands for unification replaced these earlier mottoes with sentiments such as "We Are *One* People" and "Germany One Nation," especially at the Monday demonstrations in Leipzig. . . . The majority of the population was demanding unification.

VIEWPOINT 3

A Journey of Celebration

Andreas Ramos

Although East Germany lifted its border restrictions, and opened the gates of the Berlin Wall, on the night of November 9 through 10, 1989, the celebrations continued for days afterward. In the following selection, writer and Internet expert Andreas Ramos recounts a journey that he took from his home in Denmark to Germany, accompanied by his wife and two friends. They left Denmark by car on November 11, wanting to see and take part in the massive changes underway in Germany.

Ramos notes how, all along the way to Berlin, celebrations were underway. People from other European countries joined the East and West Germans at their national border, and many of them, like Ramos and his companions, wanted to make their way to Berlin. Ramos remembers that, in the city itself, crowds still filled the streets as the Berlin Wall itself was being dismantled by happy citizens. He notes furthermore that it was remarkable to be on the scene as East Germany collapsed and as history was made.

Andreas Ramos is the author or coauthor of such books as *Search Engine Marketing* and *Hands-On Web Design*. He maintains the andreas.com Web site.

SOURCE. Andreas Ramos, "A Personal Account of The Fall of the Berlin Wall: The 11th and 12th of November, 1989," *www.andreas.com*, 1989. © Andreas Ramos 1989. Reproduced by permission.

On Thursday, the 9th of November, 1989, and Friday the 10th, the TV and radio in Denmark were filled with news about the events in Berlin. The Berlin Wall was about to fall. On Saturday morning, the 11th of November, I heard on the radio that East Germany was collapsing. At the spur of the moment, I suggested to Karen, my Danish wife, and two Danish friends, Rolf Reitan and Nana Kleist, that we should go to Berlin. We talked about what one should take to a revolution: it was a very cold, dry November day. We settled on a dozen boiled eggs, a thermos pot of coffee, extra warm clothes, sleeping bags, and a battery-powered radio. The four of us packed into my 25-year-old Volkswagen bug and we drove off.

It's normally an eight-hour drive from Aarhus, Denmark, to Berlin. We took the Autobahn down to Hamburg and then across one of the transit routes

Even massive traffic jams at the border could not dim jubilance over the wall's demise on November 9, 1989. **(AP Images.)**

to Berlin. Berlin is in the center of East Germany. There are only three highways which allow access from West Germany. At the border city of Braunschweig (Brunswick), on the German side, we began to see the first Trabants. These are small East German cars. They don't just look like toy cars, they look like Donald Duck's car. It was designed by a famous East German industrial designer during the '50s and it never changed. It's the only car in the world with tail fins. It has cheap, thin metal that rusts easily. The two-stroke engine buzzes like a lawn mower and pumps out clouds of smoke. God help you if you're standing near one. Trabants, which Germans call Trabis, have a top speed of about 50 miles an hour.

After a pizza in Braunschweig, we drove towards the German/German border. It was about 11 P.M. at night now. The traffic began to slow down. Soon there was very heavy traffic. In the distance there was a tremendous cloud of light. No one knew what was going on. On the radio, reports followed one another, contradicting each other. Soon, we began to pass cars that were parked along both sides of the Autobahn. People were walking along, all heading towards the border.

> "We met people from Belgium, France, Sweden, Spain, England: they had all left their homes and come to see the wall be torn down."

We finally reached the border just after midnight. The East German border was always a serious place. Armed guards kept you in your car, watching for attempts at escapes. Tonight was a different country. Over 20,000 East and West Germans were gathered there in a huge party: as each Trabi came through, people cheered and clapped. East Germans drove through the applause, grinning, dazed, as thousands of flashbulbs went off. The traffic jam was spectacular. The cloud of light turned out to be the headlights of tens of thousands of cars in a huge cloud of Trabi exhaust fumes. We got out of the car and began walking. Between lanes of cars, streams of people were walking, talking together. Under one light, a group of musicians were playing violins and accordions and men and women were dancing in circles. Despite the brilliantly cold night, car windows were open and everyone talked to each other.

A Crowded but Happy Checkpoint

We met people from Belgium, France, Sweden, Spain, England: they had all left their homes and come to see the wall be torn down. Germans were drunk with joy. Everyone spoke in all sorts of languages and half languages. French spoke German and Spaniards spoke French and everyone spoke a bit of German. We walked for a while with a French family from Belgium: the mother had packed her two young daughters into the car and came to see the German revolution.

Along with everyone else headed towards Berlin were thousands of East Germans; they had been in West Europe for a blitz tour with the kids and grandmother in the back, to look around and drive back again. Without passports, they had simply driven through the borders. Amused West European border guards let them pass. They smiled and waved to everyone.

At the checkpoint, which is a 25-lane place, people milled around. It was nearly 3 A.M. by now. It had taken us three hours to go through the traffic jam of cheering and applause. West Germans are environmentally conscious and if they're stuck in traffic, they turn off the engine and push their cars. East Germans, on the other hand, sat in their Trabis, putting out clouds of exhaust. Everyone had their radios on and everywhere was music. People had climbed up into trees, signs, buildings, everything, to wave and shout. Television teams stood around filming everything. People set up folding tables and were handing out cups of coffee. A Polish engineer and his wife had run out of gas; someone gave us some rope, so we tied the rope to his car and pulled them along.

We walked through the border. On both sides the guard towers were empty and the barbed wire was shoved aside in great piles. Large signs told us that we needed sets of car documents. The East German guard asked if we had documents. I handed him my Danish cat's vaccination documents, in Danish. He waved us through.

We were finally inside East Germany on the transit highway to Berlin. We could see headlights stretching into the distance, a river of light winding through hills and valleys as far as one could see. We counted our odometer and saw that in the opposite direction both lanes were filled and stopped for 35 kilometers. We counted people and cars for a kilometer and guessed that perhaps another one hundred thousand people were headed westward towards West Germany.

> I knocked chunks of rubble from the wall, dropping several handfuls into my pocket.

It Was All Berlin

We drove along, listening to the radio. The only thing was Berlin. Reporters went back and forth, describing the events on the streets and where people had gathered at the wall. There were reports of shoving and arrests. Large crowds were beginning to form into mobs. Police stood around. There were reports of rumor of soldiers and military vehicles, both East and West. At one point in the wall, the crowd had begun to tear down the wall. They succeeded in carrying away a 3-meter-tall slab.

We arrived in Berlin at 4:30 A.M., five hours longer than usual. We drove first to Brandenburgerplatz, where the statute of Winged Victory stands atop a 50 meter column, which celebrates a military victory in the 1890s over Denmark. Cars were abandoned everywhere, wherever there was space. Over 5,000 people were there.

I began talking to people. We left the car and began to walk through a village of television trucks, giant satellite dishes, emergency generators, and coils of cables, and tents. Cameramen slept under satellite dishes. At the wall, West German police and military were lined up to prevent chaos. West German military trucks were lined up against the wall, to protect it from the West Germans. Hundreds of West German police stood in rows with their tall shields. On top of the wall, lined up at parade rest, stood East German soldiers with their rifles. Groups of West Germans stood around fires that they had built. No one knew what was going on.

After a while, we walked to Potsdamer Platz. This used to be the center of Berlin. All traffic once passed through the Potsdamer Platz. Now it was a large empty field, bisected by the wall. Nearby was the mound that was the remains of Hitler's bunker, from which he commanded Germany into total defeat. We talked to Germans and many said that the next break in the wall would be here. It was still very dark and cold at 5 A.M. Perhaps 7,000 people were pressed together, shouting, cheering, clapping. We pushed through the crowd. From the East German side we could hear the sound of heavy machines. With a giant drill, they were punching holes in the wall. Every time a drill poked through, everyone cheered. The banks of klieg lights would come on. People shot off fireworks and emergency flares and rescue rockets. Many were using hammers to chip away at the wall. There were countless holes. At one place, a crowd of East German soldiers looked through a narrow hole. We reached through and shook hands. They couldn't see the crowd, so they asked us what was going on and we described the scene for them. Someone lent me a hammer and I knocked chunks of rubble from the wall, dropping several handfuls into my pocket. The wall was made of cheap, brittle concrete: the Russians had used too much sand and water.

Freedom to Cross Borders

Progress seemed rather slow and we figured it'd take another hour. The car wouldn't start anymore without a push. We went back towards the city for coffee or beer or whatever. We drove down the Kurfurstendamm (the Ku'damm), the central boulevard. Hundreds of thousands of people were walking around, going in and out of stores, looking around, drinking cheap East German champagne. Thousands of champagne bottles littered the streets. Thousands of Trabis were parked wherever they had found a space, between trees, between park benches, on traffic islands. Everything was open: restaurants, bars, discos, everything. Yesterday over two million East Germans had entered Berlin. The radio reported that over 100,000 were entering every hour. With Berlin's population of three million, there were over five million people milling around in delirious joy celebrating the reunion of the city after 28 years (Aug. 12, 1961–Nov. 9, 1989). A newspaper wrote banner headlines: Germany is reunited in the streets!

The East German government was collapsing. East German money was worthless. West Germany gave every East German 100 Deutschmark, which amounted to several months wages. The radio announced that banks and post offices would open at 9 A.M. so that the people could pick up their cash with a stamp in their identification papers. Thousands stood in line.

We left our car in front of the [Gedäctnis Kirche], the Church of Remembrance, bombed-out ruins of a church, left as a memorial to the victims of the war.

We walked into a bar. Nearly everything was sold out. A huge crowd was talking and laughing all at once. We found a table. An old woman came up and asked if we were Germans. We said no, Danish, and invited her and her family to our table. We shared chairs and beer. They were East Germans, mother, father, and daughter. She worked in a factory, her husband was a plumber, and the daughter worked in a shop. They came from a small village several hundred kilometers to the south. The old woman said that she had last seen Berlin 21 years ago and couldn't recognize it. They told us about the chaos of the last few weeks. I asked them what they had bought in Berlin. They all pulled out their squirt guns. They thought it was so funny to fill up the squirt guns with beer and shoot at everybody. The family had chased a cat in an alley and eaten a dinner of bananas, a luxury for them. We talked about movies; they knew the directors and cameramen. The father was very happy at the idea of being able to travel. He wanted to go to Peru and see Machu Picchu and then to Egypt and see the pyramids. They had no desire to live in the West. They knew about unemployment and drug problems. Their apartment rent was $2 a month. A bus ticket cost less than a penny.

> "Looking around, I saw an indescribable joy in people's faces."

At seven A.M. or so, we left and headed back to the Potsdamer Platz. Old Volkswagens don't have gas gauges. The car ran out of gas. Someone said that there was a gas station five blocks ahead. People joined us in pushing the car to the gas station. When we arrived, people were standing around. The electricity had failed in the neighborhood so the gas pumps were dead. The owner shrugged at the small bother and waved us towards the coffee. Dozens of East Germans, young, old, children, stood around drinking coffee. After an hour or so, the electricity came on and we filled up the tank. With a crowd of people, we pushed the car up and down the street three times to get it to start. We drove back to Potsdamer Platz.

Knocking Down the Wall

Everything was out of control. Police on horses watched. There was nothing they could do. The crowd had swol-

> At the border, there were no guards anymore.

len. People were blowing long alpine horns which made a huge noise. There were fireworks, kites, flags and flags and flags, dogs, children. The wall was finally breaking. The cranes lifted slabs aside. East and West German police had traded caps. To get a better view, hundreds of people were climbing onto a shop on the West German side. We scampered up a nine-foot wall. People helped each other; some lifted, others pulled. All along the building, people poured up the wall. At the Berlin Wall itself, which is 3 meters high, people had climbed up and were sitting astride. The final slab was moved away. A stream of East Germans began to pour through. People applauded and slapped their backs. A woman handed me a giant bottle of wine, which I opened and she and I began to pour cups of wine and hand them to the East Germans. Journalists and TV reporters struggled to hold their cameras. A foreign news agency's van with TV cameras on top was in a crowd of people; it rocked and the cameramen pleaded with the crowd. Packed in with thousands, I stood at the break in the wall. Above me, a German stood atop the wall, at the end, balanced, waving his arms and shouting reports to the crowd. With all of the East Germans coming into West Berlin, we thought it was only fair that we should go to East Berlin. A counter-flow started. Looking around, I saw an indescribable joy in people's faces. It was the end of the government telling people what not to do, it was the end of the Wall, the war, the East, the West. If East Germans were going west, then we should go east, so we poured into East Berlin. Around me, people spoke German, French, Polish, Russian, every language. A woman handed her camera to someone who was standing atop rubble so that he could take her picture. I passed a group of American reporters; they didn't speak anything and couldn't understand what was going on, pushing their microphones into people's faces, asking, "Do you speak English?" Near me, a knot of people cheered as the mayors of East Berlin and West Berlin met and shook hands. I stood with several East German guards, their rifles slung over their shoulders. I asked them if they had bullets in those things. They grinned and said no. From some houses, someone had set up loudspeakers and played Beethoven's Ninth Symphony: *Alle Menschen werden Brüder*. "All people become brothers." On top of every building were thousands of people. Berlin was out of control. There was no more government, neither in East nor in West. The police and the army were helpless. The soldiers themselves were overwhelmed by the event. They were part of the crowd. Their uniforms meant nothing. The Wall was down.

After a while, we left and went back to the city, to find some food. The TV was set to East German TV. The broadcasters began showing whatever they wanted: roving cameras in the street, film clips, porno, speeches from parliament, statements, videos, nature films, live interviews. West Berliners went out of their homes and brought East Germans in for food and rest. A friend of ours in Berlin had two families sleeping in her living room. The radio told that in Frankfurt, a Trabi had been hit by a Mercedes. Nothing happened to the Mercedes but the Trabi was destroyed. A crowd of people collected money for the East German family; the driver of the Mercedes gave them her keys and lent them her car for the weekend. A West German went home, got his truck, and drove the Trabi back to East Germany. Late Sunday, the West German government declared on radio and TV that East Germans had free access to all public transportation: buses, streetcars, and trains, plus free admission to all zoos, museums, concerts, practically everything. More than 80% of East Germany was on vacation in West Germany, nearly 13 million people, visiting family and friends in the West. After a week, nearly all returned home.

After a dinner of spaghetti, we got back into the Volkswagen and headed home. The radio talked about delays of ten hours, but then again, that was just another rumor. At the border, there were no guards anymore. Late the next morning, we were back in Denmark.

VIEWPOINT 4

Memorable Scenes in Central Berlin

Henry Porter

British reporter Henry Porter, the author of the following selection, was one of the thousands of journalists who traveled to Berlin in November 1989 to report on the fall of the Berlin Wall. The following selection is from a commemorative article he wrote for the 10th anniversary of the event in 1999.

Porter remembers that, despite celebrations in various parts of Berlin, there was still a great deal of uncertainty the night of November 9, when East German border restrictions were lifted. He recalls that at one point, walking through East Berlin, he grew afraid that he might be "trapped in the east without papers" when he and his companion came across the confused border guards. On November 10, he notes, reporters had gathered from around the world while the border guards themselves had given up the pretense of restrictions to join ordinary people in knocking down the wall. Throughout, and with the benefit of 10 years' hindsight, Porter remembers the experience of being in Berlin in November 1989 with a historical perspective going back through the Cold War to the Nazi era of World

---

SOURCE. Henry Porter, "Drink! Dance! It's All Over!" *The Guardian (UK)*, November 3, 1999. Copyright © 1999 Guardian Newspapers Limited. Reproduced by permission of Guardian News Service, LTD.

War II. Among his observations was that not all West Berliners were joyful about their new world.

Henry Porter writes on intelligence and international affairs for the *Guardian* newspaper in Great Britain. He has written four novels and the nonfiction book *Lies, Damned Lies*.

I reached up to the top of the wall and hands came down to meet mine out of the darkness. I grabbed them and pulled myself up, then wriggled over the edge on my stomach. Suddenly I was looking down on East Berlin, a wide open space in front of the Brandenburg Gate in which several military vehicles, a water cannon and about 50 border guards waited. The Brandenburg rose behind them huge and illuminated, like a piece of opera scenery. Beyond was the darkness of East Berlin. It was sometime in the middle of the night of November 9. At 6:55 PM that evening, the East German government had lifted all travel restrictions to the west and in effect announced the demise of the Berlin Wall. But at that moment it was unbreached, its aura of menace still very much intact. One felt a strong sense of trespass on top of the wall. I couldn't see much of what was happening beyond no man's land, the exclusion zone of mines and barbed wire on the east. Most of the East Germans who had dropped everything to make use of the relaxed travel restrictions were flowing through the checkpoints; the few that had broken through at the Brandenburg had been herded back by the Grenzpolizei [border police] or had taken refuge on top of the wall.

> It was not enough just to make light of the wall. It had to be smashed.

A Great Exhilaration

On the western side, however, one was aware of great exhilaration, a mood which consisted of anger, joy, disbelief, defiance and urgency. It was plain everyone understood that something undreamt of and enormous was happening. From our vantage point we watched and gaped, each person shivering in the presence of what I suppose was raw history.

In front of the Brandenburg, the wall measured four feet across, so there was enough room for hundreds of people to stand, drink and jeer down at the border guards. But it was not enough just to make light of the wall. It had to be smashed. There was a steady chinking of claw hammers, axes, crowbars and picks which were wielded with a ferocious, maniacal rhythm, each blow sending tiny shards of concrete into the air, although doing little actual damage.

The faces of the Grenzpolizei, the hated Grepos, showed puzzlement and outrage. The structure that had defined the GDR [German Democratic Republic, or East Germany], delineated its society, the thing they had patrolled with almost religious zeal, was under attack from the degenerates of both sides. For the first time in nearly 30 years, they were powerless to stop the desecration of what [former East German leader] Erich Honecker once called "the anti-fascist defence wall". You could see they found this hard to bear, these goons still dressed in their thin summer uniforms. What they'd give to shoot a few dozen rounds into the mob was anyone's guess. But they had new orders, and their weapons remained lowered.

They did, however, have the water cannon, and aimed jets at demonstrators causing them to drop on all fours. One or two rose and stood against the water, arms outstetched with victory salutes to the crowds that were building in Tiergarten, the huge park on the west side. One man in a leather jacket stood for several minutes unaware of the halo formed by the illuminated spray bouncing off his back. He just smiled and slowly raised his arms outwards. The crowd roared and whistled and the hairs on the back of my neck rose as I turned and watched the faces, all utterly unself-conscious and absorbed in this extraordinary moment.

Students lowered themselves into the east and ran around performing Chaplinesque antics on the bright stage in front of the Brandenburg. Someone else produced firecrackers; little Chinese rockets were aimed down at the water cannon. Women beseeched guards: Come up here! Drink! Dance! It's all over! Forget the damned wall! Forget the GDR!

> In the morning, the wall was still being patrolled. But the game was clearly up.

Quiet in the East

Late at night, myself and Carl, a tall, quiet engineering student who had driven me from the Tempelhof airport in the taxi he used to pay his way through college, went into the east. A guard demanded to know what we were doing. "We're going home," Carl returned coolly. And so we walked past the Brandenburg and up Unter der Linden (Under the Lime Trees) into the dark, almost deserted east. There was no traffic, lights were few and there was no sign of the million people who demonstrated in Alexanderplatz on November 4 for the right to govern their own lives. They were all in bed, Carl surmised: they would be going to their jobs later that day.

We turned down Wilhemstrasse, a ley line linking Nazi sites. Somewhere out to our right was the low tumulus which is all that is visible of Hitler's bunker. Two years later, I returned and found the exact spot where Hitler signed his last will and testament, in which he described himself as essentially a peace-loving leader, a man who had been undone by the conspiracy of international Jewry. It was of course mere fancy, but somehow the ghosts of Berlin's war seemed to have been released that night in the echoing, empty streets.

We passed [Nazi air commander Hermann] Goering's air ministry, the building that had survived 45,000 tons of

Allied bombs, and looked up at the communist mural in the entrance: muscular types raising banners and bearing wheatsheafs; children in headscarves, rosy-faced, fecund, labouring women. And then on to where Himmler's headquarters had stood. We did not know then, no one did, that under the wasteland between the street and the wall lay the cells in which Nazi victims were tortured.

As we walked, the noise of the crowd at the Brandenburg seemed to float on the wind and fade. I think both of us were suddenly gripped by the irrational fear that this was just an episode and that we would be trapped in the east without papers. We hurried back to the Brandenburg, and were stopped by a guard who again demanded where we were going. "That's okay, we're just going home," said Carl again, this time placing a comradely hand on the guard's shoulder. He didn't like it, but we passed back into the west.

Early Signals

In the morning, the wall was still being patrolled. But the game was clearly up. [East German Communist] Egon Krenz's East German government was in disarray. Ten years later, we tend to think of the collapse of the communist regimes as coming like a bolt from blue, but there had been signals. The Soviet president, Mikhail Gorbachev, and his foreign minister, Edvard Shevardnadze, had hinted all year that the Iron Curtain might come down. In January 1989, the month the last person was killed on the wall, Shevardnadze said: "The wall was built under particular circumstances. We must carefully examine if those circumstances still apply."

You could hardly be less oblique, but the East German authorities never listened. Krenz, the former security chief who had replaced Honecker 25 days before, didn't seem to hear the voices of 300,000 people who demonstrated when he acquired the title Head of the National Defence Council; he took no notice of the flood of East

Germans leaving for the West through Czechoslovakia and Hungary. So many had gone during the summer that the army had to help run public transport. Looking back now, it seems obvious the whole country was collapsing in slow motion. Yet the final spasms were so abrupt and vivid they took everyone by surprise.

November 10 was a sharp, sunlit day. Carl and I spent most of the morning drinking and walking up and down the wall. The US news networks had arrived. Dan Rather was anchoring a programme from the new Germany with the Brandenburg and the wall behind him. The crowd had swollen. Equipped with sledgehammers and pick-axes, people were bumping into each other in Tiergarten, squealing with delight and shouting slogans. Near the Potsdamer Platz, where the wall consisted of concrete slabs just a few inches thick, holes had appeared. There were rumours that diggers had been moved up by the East Germans and that the border guards had joined in to knock down the first slabs.

I never tired of watching Germans fall into each other's arms. We climbed up on the wall again, where there was more furious activity. The atmosphere was far more giddy and joyous than on the previous night. [Poet William] Wordsworth's couplet came to mind: "Bliss it was in that dawn to be alive, but to be young was very heaven." And it was the young who were in the vanguard of the demonstrations in East Berlin and Leipzig; and it was students who soon took the fight against oppression to the streets in Prague, Timisoara and Bucharest. People have forgotten how bold they were and the debt that democracy in the east owes them.

"A large proportion of West Berlin ignored what was going on."

Pensive East Germans

Of course, on that penetratingly cold evening, most East Germans did not want to linger by the wall. Once they had passed through the checkpoints, they left for the bright lights and department stores, some puttering along in little Trabant cars, others walking briskly. They were instantly identifiable as many wore the stonewashed pale blue denim that had been fashionable in the west four years before. They seemed a little lost. They had only seen such wealth and abundance on TV, but even though their faces were pressed to the windows of the stores they were no nearer to acquiring them: East German marks were almost worthless in the west.

So they drifted about looking overawed, cold and slightly resentful. Occasionally West Berliners would greet them, but it was my impression that the westerners were now thinking about the downside of the wall's collapse: the cost, the political upheaval and the effort that would be required to harmonise two totally different systems. To say joy was the universal emotion in West Berlin would be wrong. A large proportion of West Berlin ignored what was going on.

I bumped into a friend and we went to look at Checkpoint Charlie. We walked through, chatting to disconsolate guards. The penny had dropped with them: no wall meant no jobs. The demands of the frontier and its elaborate, needy fabric, together with the security it had given them, had vanished. A decade on we've forgotten the mystique of the wall, not just its meaning to the west, where it was regarded as the edge of civilisation. In the east, the Iron Curtain was officially a secret. It wasn't mentioned in the press and its minefields, fortifications and observation towers were never referred to. People knew it existed—they could hardly fail to notice—but they did not acknowledge it.

Varied Signs of Change

We walked everywhere, watching whole slabs of the wall crash down, seeing flurries of celebration, awkward reunions, people falling silent. Then dawn came up. Carl and I breakfasted groggily on brandy, coffee and

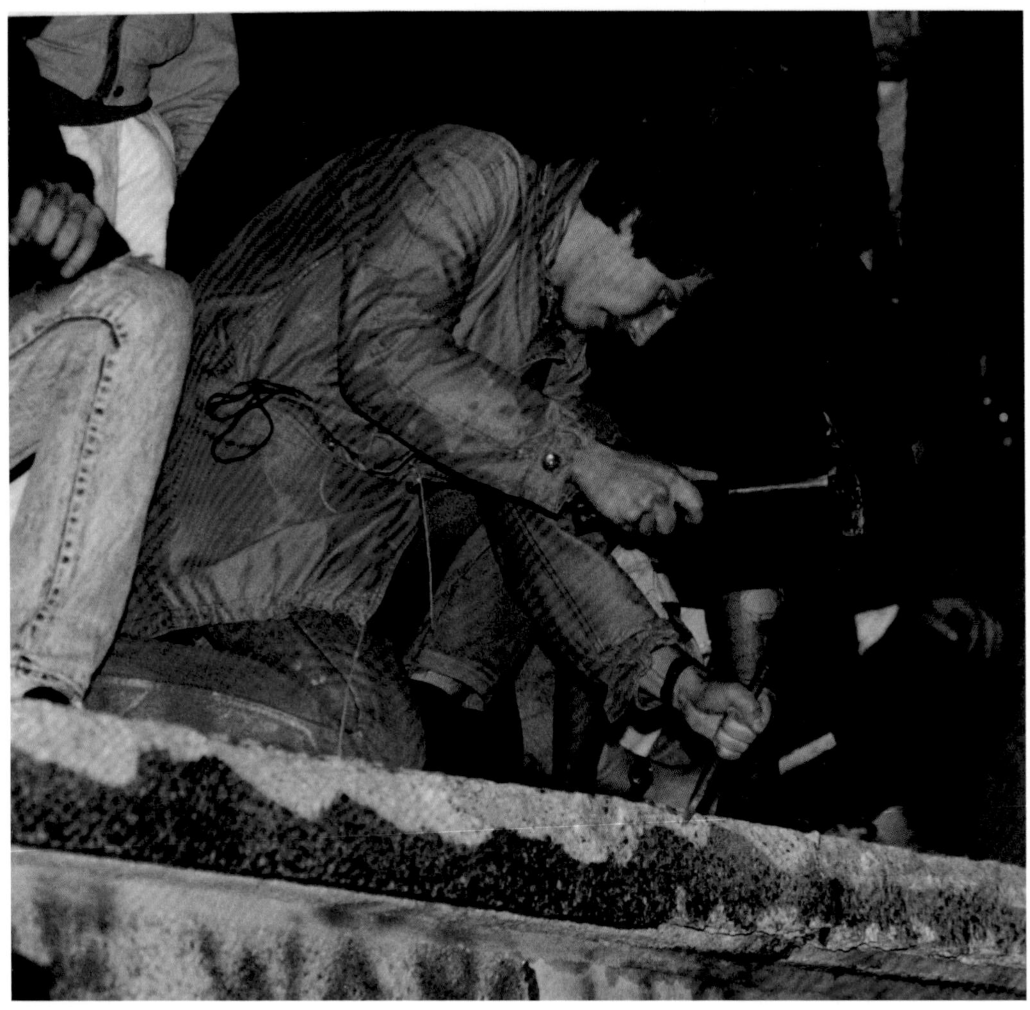

Many people took pieces of the Berlin Wall as souvenirs on the night border restrictions were lifted. (AP Images.)

pastries outside a cafe, under a crystal blue sky. It was Saturday, November 11, 71 years to the day since the guns fell silent on the western front. At that time, I had no real perspective on the events I was witnessing, but it soon became clear that a lot of the century's business, and a dreadful period in Germany's history, was being concluded.

I noticed trucks from a chain of supermarkets had suddenly materialised along the wall. Someone had had the weird idea of giving East Berliners a bag of sugar as they emerged from new crossing points. Queues had formed. You couldn't doubt the genuineness of the gesture or that it met some kind of need, but a kilogramme bag of sugar didn't seem quite equal to the occasion.

That afternoon we drove to the Glienicker Bridge, an austere iron structure over the River Havel where many exchanges took place during the cold war. In 1962, U2 pilot Gary Powers was swapped for the master spy Ivanovitch Abel; and on a frosty day in February 1986, Anatol Scharansky, the persecuted Jewish lawyer, walked to freedom over the bridge. The Havel sparkled below us. An East German rowing eight was at practice. They stopped and looked up at the traffic passing over the bridge, hundreds of little cars flowing into the west, pedestrians being greeted by women with flowers and hugs.

"The wall no longer existed in any meaningful way."

The rowers mopped their brows and shook their heads. And then from nowhere a shiny green Huey US helicopter came to hover above the western side of the Havel. The thump of its rotor added a deafening, cinematic glamour to the scene and a downdraft caught the trees and spilled a mass of yellow leaves into the Havel. Everyone looked up and waved to the US civilians standing in the open door of the Huey. They waved back and a huge cheer rose from Glienicker. It was that moment, with its visible emanations of hope, its movement, noise and vivid autumn colours, that has stayed most clearly imprinted in my mind.

We drove back to the town centre. The wall no longer existed in any meaningful way. Afterwards, I reflected that if it had not been built there would never have been such a swift and dramatic end to the tyranny in the east. Just as its existence had terrorised the people of the GDR, its destruction provided an absolute and categoric symbol of their liberation.

VIEWPOINT 5

Looking Back and Looking Forward on the Tenth Anniversary of the Wall's Collapse

Doris Bergen

The following selection is historian Doris Bergen's note of both celebration and thoughtfulness on the tenth anniversary of the fall of the Berlin Wall in November 1999. As Bergen indicates, she was living in West Berlin when the wall came down, but she traveled through the wall to East Berlin every day to conduct research. And despite hints of changes and news of large-scale protests, she remembers being surprised at hearing of the end of East Germany's border restrictions.

Ten years later, she plans a small commemorative celebration and has no regrets for the end of East Germany. But she also wants to caution readers against being too self-satisfied and triumphant about the wall's end being the symbol of a Western victory in the Cold War. History, she writes, is unpredict-

---

SOURCE. Doris Bergen, "The Fall of the Berlin Wall and the Surprises of History," *Observer* (Notre Dame), vol. XXXIII, November 9, 1999. Reproduced by permission.

able and no event is inevitable. She urges a sense of humility and an attempt at a truer and deeper understanding of the meaning of such great events as the fall of the Berlin Wall and the end of European communism.

Doris Bergen is a professor of history and Holocaust studies at the University of Toronto.

> There was a kind of confusion and wonderment to the events of November 1989.

I find it hard to believe that 10 years have gone by since the events now known as "the fall of the Berlin Wall."

Of course the Wall didn't really fall in November 1989, nor, for that matter, did it come down. Instead, it simply and suddenly stopped being a wall, in the sense of a border and a barrier, and became something quite different: a place to party, the source of "hew-it yourself" souvenirs; a giant, international photo-opportunity—even a dance floor.

I remember it all very well, because in the fall of 1989, I was living in Berlin (West), finishing up the research for my Ph.D. dissertation. I had spent much of September and October commuting every day from my cheap but trendy neighborhood to an archive in Potsdam, across the border in East Germany. The trip took three hours and four forms of public transportation each way. It included a stop at the border that could take anywhere from 10 minutes to two hours, and involve anything from an order to reveal my right ear and remove my glasses to a full body search. Later I would discover that the archive in Potsdam was only 20 minutes by car from my flat in Berlin-Schoeneberg.

But in September and October 1989, it felt worlds away. So I didn't expect to emerge from a long day of research on Nov. 9, 1989, to see the security guards at the archive gathered around their radio, weeping.

"What's going on?" I asked.

"They're dancing on the Wall!" one of them told me.

History Is Complex

History, I discovered in the fall of 1989, is not predictable. Nor is it inevitable, simple or unambiguous. I was surprised by the events of Nov. 9, 1989, but I was not uninformed. Like everyone in Berlin, I had become addicted to news sometime that spring and summer. So much was happening all around us—in Poland, Hungary, the Soviet Union, next door in the German Democratic Republic and as far away as China. My housemate and I bought every newspaper we could find—and took every opportunity we could to get on a train or plane—to see for ourselves.

During 1989, I visited Yugoslavia and Poland, the Soviet Union and Czechoslovakia each twice and East Germany more times than I could count. I knew that those countries were being transformed—anyone could see that—but I had no idea that within a few years, all of them, except for Poland, would have ceased to exist. As late as October 1989, it seemed as likely that East Germany would be the site of another crackdown in the style of [China's] Tiananmen Square than that the Wall would open peacefully and the two Germanies unify within a year. There was a kind of confusion and wonderment to the events of November 1989, as developments somehow took everyone by surprise. For me, that air of bemused joy will always be associated with the hordes of East German cars—small, stinky Trabants—that poured across the border in the late weeks of 1989. Their drivers had no idea where they were going; East German maps included only white space in what was West Berlin.

Not Necessarily an American Victory

It's easy to be smart—and smug—looking back from our vantage point a decade later. It's also easy to forget that in November 1989, the opening of the Berlin Wall didn't look like the final American victory in the Cold War. Instead it looked like the triumph of a few daring leaders and a lot of peaceful, persistent protesters in the countries of the east bloc, from the Soviet Union to Poland, Hungary, Czechoslovakia and the German Democratic Republic.

Today, 10 years later, Mikhail Gorbachev—once renowned architect of *glasnost* and idol of Germans east and west—has long been reduced to making advertisements for Pizza Hut. The women and men who faced down police to demand "socialism with a human face" are all but forgotten, buried beneath a few CNN clips of euphoric, champagne-swilling crowds dancing on the Wall. Maybe there is another lesson about history here, a lesson about how quickly and effortlessly we rewrite the past to suit our needs in the present.

I'm not nostalgic about the disappearance of the East German state. It was an oppressive, dishonest, destructive regime based on a network of informants so dense that they outnumbered the objects of surveillance in many dissident organizations. It was a paranoid regime too, with its watchtowers, dogs and armies of petty bureaucrats eager to regulate and obstruct. Even the food was terrible, at least what you could get easily as a visitor in shops and restaurants. Nor do I mourn the collapse of communism, a system that took an enormous toll on members of my own family in Ukraine in the 1920s and 1930s, and later in Siberia.

My only plea is for some humility in the face of history and its complexity. By all means, celebrate the tenth anniversary of the fall of the Wall. I intend to raise a glass myself, but keep in mind the generations of people whose lives and struggles, past and present, can be obscured by the easy claim that "we won the Cold War."

CHRONOLOGY

1871 Berlin is named the capital of the newly united German state.

1933 Berlin is reinvented as the capital of Adolf Hitler's Nazi state.

1945 Both Germany and Berlin are divided into four zones of occupation following the defeat of Nazi Germany and the end of World War II.

1948 The Soviet Union blockades Berlin beginning in June. The Western powers successfully supply their three sectors of Berlin in the Berlin airlift, forcing the lifting of the Soviet blockade in May 1949.

1949 The founding of the democratic Federal Republic of Germany (West Germany) occurs in May.

The founding of the Communist German Democratic Republic (East Germany) occurs in October.

1953 Border crossings between East and West Germany are closed. Those in Berlin remain open.

1958 The Soviet Union demands that the Western powers leave Berlin. They refuse.

1959 Some 144,000 people escape East Germany through West Berlin.

In September Soviet and American leaders agree that

the Berlin conflict should be settled through negotiation, not force.

1961 In June Soviet leaders demand that the Western powers leave Berlin within six months. They refuse.

In the month of July alone, thirty thousand people escape through West Berlin.

East German leaders announce new border restrictions on August 13 and start to build the Berlin Wall.

The United States increases its military preparedness over the possible need to defend West Berlin.

1962 In August, 18-year-old Peter Fechter is shot trying to escape across the Berlin Wall and is among the first of many to die in the attempt.

In October the Cuban missile crisis shifts the focus of the Cold War away from Berlin.

1963 U.S. President John F. Kennedy makes his "I am a Berliner" speech on June 26.

1963 In December West Berliners may get special permits to visit East Berlin.

1971 A new four-power agreement eases travel restrictions and establishes new ties between East and West Berlin.

1987 On June 12 U.S. President Ronald Reagan makes a Berlin speech in which he asks the Soviet Union to "tear down this wall."

1988 In December Soviet leader Mikhail Gorbachev announces the drawdown of longstanding Soviet forces in Eastern Europe.

1989 Hungary lifts its border restrictions with Austria in August, providing an escape route for East Germans.

In September East Germans protest, demanding democratic reforms.

On October 18 longstanding East German leader Erich Honecker resigns.

On November 4 more than one million East Germans protest in Berlin's Alexanderplatz public square.

On November 9 East German leaders announce the end of internal border restrictions.

The Berlin Wall falls between November 9 and 10.

1990 On October 3 Germany is reunited.

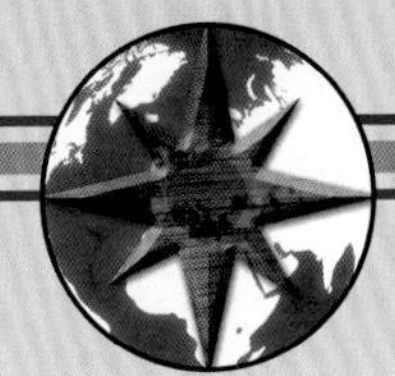

FOR FURTHER READING

Books

Joel Agee, *Twelve Years: An American Boyhood in East Germany*. New York: Farrar, Straus, and Giroux, 1981.

John Ardagh, *Germany and the Germans*. London: Penguin, 1987.

John Borneman, *After the Wall: East Meets West in the New Berlin*. New York: Basic Books, 1991.

Andrei Cherny, *The Candy Bombers: The Untold Story of the Berlin Airlift and America's Finest Hour*. New York: G.P. Putnam's Sons/Penguin, 2008.

Richard Crockatt, *The Fifty Years War: The United States and the Soviet Union in World Politics, 1941–1991*. New York: Routledge, 1994.

Robert Darnton, *Berlin Journal, 1989–1990*. New York: Norton, 1991.

Dinah Dodds and Pam Allen-Thompson, *The Wall in My Backyard*. Amherst: University of Massachusetts Press, 1994.

John Lewis Gaddis, *We Now Know: Rethinking Cold War History*. Oxford, UK: Oxford University Press, 1997.

Peter Gay, *My German Question*. New Haven, CT: Yale University Press, 1998.

Mikhail Gorbachev, *Perestroika: New Thinking for Our Country and the World*. New York: Harper and Row, 1987.

Katie Hafner, *The House at the Bridge: A Story of Modern Germany*. New York: Scribner, 1995.

Louis J. Halle, *The Cold War as History*. New York: Harper Torchbooks, 1967.

Christopher Hilton, *The Wall: The People's Story*. Gloucestershire, UK: Sutton, 2001.

Konrad H. Jarausch, *The Rush to German Unity*. New York: Oxford University Press, 1994.

Anthony Kemp, *Escape from Berlin*. London, Boxtree Ltd., 1987.

Anne McElvoy, *The Saddled Cow: East Germany's Life and Legacy*. London: Faber and Faber, 1991.

Norman M. Naimark, *The Russians in Germany*. Cambridge, MA: Harvard University Press, 1995.

James P. O'Donnell, *The Berlin Bunker*. London: Arrow Books, 1979.

Dirk Philipsen. *We Were the People*. Durham, NC: Duke University Press, 1993.

Anthony Read and David Fisher, *The Fall of Berlin*. London, Hutchinson, 1992.

Peter Schneider, *The German Comedy: Scenes of Life After the Wall*. New York: Farrar, Straus, and Giroux, 1991.

Ken Smith, *Berlin: Coming in from the Cold*. London: Hamish Hamilton, 1990.

Anne Tusa and John Tusa, *The Berlin Airlift*. New York: Atheneum, 1988.

Martin Walker, *The Cold War: A History*. New York: Henry Holt, 1993.

Peter Wyden, *Wall: The Inside Story of Divided Berlin*. New York: Simon and Schuster, 1989.

Articles

Associated Press, "Hundreds of East Germans Find Asylum on Menu at Hungarian Picnic," *Boston Globe*, August, 20, 1989.

Adrian Bridge, "Berlin: Beyond the Wall: Rise and Fall of the Wall," *Independent* (UK), November 9, 1994.

"Freedom!" *Time*, November 20, 1989.

Cline Freeman, "The World Rejoices as Berlin Wall Falls," *Charleston Gazette*, November 11, 1989.

John Hamer, "The Party Atmosphere Is Over," *Seattle Times*, June 7, 1990.

James O. Jackson, "Unity's Shadow," *Time*, July 1, 1991.

Stephen Kinzer, "Where Is Optimism in Germany? Among the Bedraggled Easterners." *New York Times*, December 27, 1993.

Tyler Marshall, "New Wall Goes Up in Germany," *Los Angeles Times*, August 20, 1992.

Elizabeth Pongratz, "Berlin Today: Rebirth and Reunification." *Seattle Times*, November 9, 1999.

"Soul Searching at 40: East Germany," *Economist*, October 7, 1989.

Fritz Stern, "Freedom and Its Discontents," *Foreign Affairs*, September/October, 1993.

Gary A. Warner, Five Years After the Wall Came Down, Germans Reflect on Reunification." *Orange County Register*, November 9, 1994.

"What Has the Fall of the Berlin Wall Meant to You?" *Russia Journal*, November 8, 1999.

Web Sites

Berlin Wall Online (www.dailysoft.com/berlinwall). This Web site contains stories, photographs, and links on various aspects of the Berlin Wall and its fall. It also offers information on contemporary Berlin.

The Berlin Wall (www.berlin.de/mauer/index.en.html). A section of a larger Web site dedicated to the city of Berlin with a thorough examination of the Berlin Wall's history and descriptions of such modern reminders as a Berlin Wall walking trail.

The Cold War Museum (www.coldwar.org). An online museum dedicated to the entire history of the Cold War. Offers tours, games, and other interactive resources.

INDEX

C

D

N

O

P

R